PHOENIX

PHOENIX

Therapeutic Patterns of
Milton H. Erickson

by

David Gordon and Maribeth Meyers-Anderson

International Standard Book Number: 0–916990–10–9
Library of Congress Catalog Card Number: 81–85263
Meta Publications, P.O. Box 565, Cupertino, Ca 95014

To Milton H. Erickson—
Three years and three children later, thank you.
DG and MB

TABLE OF CONTENTS

CHAPTER V—THE SNOWBALL

CHAPTER VI—SNAKE DANCE

CHAPTER VII—ORIGIN OF THE SPECIE 164

CHAPTER 1

Phoenix

Phoenix was ablaze with summer sun in June of 1978. We had just arrived at that Arizona oasis after a hot and dusty trip across the vast and shimmering deserts, and now it was utter luxury to stretch out before a clattering air-conditioner in the motel room. Only a short time before, while roasting in the car, there had been ample time to reminisce about favorite failures and successes, hopes and plans. Long distance driving somehow lends itself to such rehashing and reverie. In fact, the thorny cacti, towering mesas, and endless horizons gliding just beyond our car windows seemed to compel our internal meanderings as naturally as a needle draws its thread. The driving now done, and our view confined to the drab motel walls, each of us began to speculate privately about the great event that was now incredibly imminent.

For the previous four years we had heard, read and studied about Dr. Milton H. Erickson of Phoenix, Arizona, the world's foremost hypnotherapist. These studies had commenced with our apprenticeship to Richard Bandler and John Grinder (who have been so instrumental in making Milton Erickson's profoundly effective hypnotic patterns readily available to others), and like starvelings at a feast, we greedily consumed every written work of Erickson's on which we could lay our hands. We worked hard and made those patterns a natural part of our ongoing communications with others. And we not only used them in our own practices, but boldly traveled around the country training others in the art of Dr. Erickson's communicational alchemy. We unabashedly extolled his techniques and wisdom to all who would listen, and no doubt in our honest fervor our eyes glistened and our bodies trembled as we lectured. We talked, ate, drank, and dreamed Milton H. Erickson for years. He was family. And in making such a full confession it must be admitted that we even copied his voice . . . and we had never even MET the man! Well tomorrow we *would* meet Milton Erickson and, so, finally provide our past mimicries and expostulations with the self-flattering credence of personal contact. "Dr. Erickson? Oh yes, we know Milton . . ." But is that what this meeting was to mean? Until tomorrow we could speculate freely, while cooling our heels, courtesy of the Fedders Air-Conditioning corporation . . . But even through that filtered air we could sense in the desert wind something . . . something for which we were hardly prepared. This would be more than a culminating and confirming visit to one of those national monuments about which one has previously only read. We thought that we were coming to Phoenix to confirm what we already knew . . . and didn't know then that instead we would discover how much there was to learn. This was not to be denouement, but the introduction.

The next day we got our bearings in the cool, but already changing morning air of Phoenix. Some places go through seasonal changes two, three, or four times a year. The desert goes through five or six seasonal changes in the course of a single day. You must either adjust to those fluctuations, or hide from them. We had learned to adjust and, so, were delighted to discover the subtle changes in the appearances of colors and distance, in the feel of the air, in the timbre of sounds, and in the changing fragrances that accompanied those daily seasons.

We made our way down open, clean streets lined with orange-spotted citrus trees until we arrived at a well-planted corner house. It was neither manicured nor unkempt, but comfortable, with just the right amount of weeds and unexpected plantings so that you didn't notice that things *had* been landscaped. The yard said, "Go ahead and step on the grass, that's what it's *for.*" Each of us pushing the other to the fore, we timidly approached the front door where we were met by gracious Mrs. Erickson, who then steered us to Dr. Erickson's office. The office was small, lined with books, photographs, innumerable curious objects, and splashed with purple colors throughout. There were other pilgrims already seated in the room. We exchanged nods with them, and that seemed plenty of recognition—almost too much. Somehow we knew that this was not a social event, but personal, private. We each found our own seats and, like Indians in a sweat lodge, we all quietly waited, warming, for the medicine man to arrive and lead our devotions.

The door opens. Mrs. Erickson is at the helm of Dr. Erickson's wheel chair, and no doubt he is the only one in the room breathing at this moment. He is dressed all in purple and wears a bolo tie that sports purple cowrie shells. Despite the chromed contraption and the riot of purple, however, we are drawn immediately to his beautifully twinkling eyes, and you know that a youngster has just entered the room. A jolt! We hadn't expected that Milton H. Erickson would turn out to be the youngest person in the room. He turns his pair of twinkling search lights on each of us in turn, and you know you have been spotted. And we hadn't expected that jolt either. All of our studies and preparations seemed paltry now, and so, for now, relieved of the burden of presumption, we settled ourselves into our chairs and prepared for a *real* education. Dr. Milton H. Erickson had threaded his needle and now began to sew . . .

Now, the first consideration in dealing with patients, cli-ents or subjects is to realize that EACH of them is an *individual.* There are no two people *alike.* No two people who understand the SAME sentence the same *way,* and so in dealing with people you try not to fit them to YOUR concept of what they should *be* . . . You should try to discover what THEIR concept of themselves happens to *be* . . . I was watching a TV program on the lure of the dolphins in which scientists were trying to discover the way in which the dolphin functions, its *intelligence.* And the tendency on the part of the scientist was to anthropoMORPHIZE the dolphin . . . instead of trying to understand the dolphin as a *dolphin,* not as another form of mankind. Now, hand me that reindeer . . . Dan Goleman described it as a plain glass paperweight. He didn't

see my reindeer frozen in the iceberg . . . Now LAN-
GUAGE is not just something that is SPOKEN. And dolphins can, communicating, alter their positions of their
bodies . . . streamline their bodies in various forms in
order to communicate . . . or to *receive* communication.
And people do the same thing . . . Now how do you
manage this situation? Our daughter was on the air base
in Okinawa, a colonel's wife. It was suggested to her last
year as a pilot program that she take twenty-three dropouts in military families and have them attend school as
a pilot program to see if it could be done. And she was
given a building with a kitchen, and she was allowed to
establish her own *concept* of the school. All the dropouts
had been arrested repeatedly, guilty of rape, drug addic-
tion, theft, assault with armed weapons . . . undisciplined
refuse. They all came to see what the teacher was going
to say about the school that they were to attend. She
explained to them, they were to attend school on a voluntary basis. They had to walk or take a bus in order to
get there. Entirely voluntary. Now she *taught* the school
and she would NOT allow *anybody* to interfere with her
teachings . . . and she would expel anybody that tried to
interfere, for a day, a week, or permanently. And she laid
down the OTHER rules. "This is YOUR school. YOU *run*
the school. I *only* teach here." And, the first year she got
one student who had the worst arrest record and he
turned around and at the end of the school year he left
for the States to enter a junior college. And at the airport
this big rambunctious lad reformed . . . threw his arms
around my daughter and kissed her good-bye and shed
tears. And she said, "So I shed tears TOO. He kissed me
and cried, so I kissed him and cried." And the other
students came down and started hooting at him for crying. He turned on them *wrathfully* and said, "Anybody
will cry when they lose their BEST friend. If any of you

think you can STOP me I'll take you *on.* " So my daughter said they hugged and kissed and cried some more.

This year at the beginning of the school year, the first day, bearing in mind what happened the previous year, they all gathered to see how "old lady Elliott" (first time my daughter KNEW she was an old lady) was going to handle things. The opening day Billy said to Joe, "Joe, let's take the shelves out of the refrigerator and you lock me in, keep me there for about two minutes 'til I get a good *high,* then you release me." And so Joe obligingly locked Billy up in the ice box, a few minutes later Billy staggared out enjoying his *high* state. And went back a SECOND time . . . everybody watching including our daughter. He went back the second time, came back again and my daughter wondering what on earth she could do to *stop* that situation. She suddenly had a bright idea. She turned to the boy who was in charge of the kitchen and said, "George, are you going to let these two bums misuse your kitchen?" He said, "I sure ain't! Hey guys let's straighten out these two bums." They administered their OWN discipline. She just ordered the teaching. And two of the boys in February celebrated their FIRST *year* of being clean . . . no arrest, no drugs, no shoplifting, no misbehavior *at all*. My daughter didn't exercise any dicipline authority. She met the students at their level.

Ever since I don't know *how long*, psychiatrists and psychologists have been devising theoretical schemes, disciplines of psychotherapy. Every year the president of the American Psychological Association propounds a NEW psychological theory of human behavior. And psychiatrists have ALWAYS been propounding schools of psychotherapy. I think Freud did the worst job. Now, Freud contributed very greatly to the UNDERSTANDING of human behavior and he did a great disservice to the utilization of *understanding* human behavior. He developed a hypothetical school of thought which could be applied, according to Freud, to ALL people, of ALL ages, male or female, young or old, ALL degrees of education, in ALL cultures, in ALL situations, and at ALL times. Freud analyzed Moses, Edgar Allen Poe, Alice in Wonderland, a North Dakota farm boy, and he wouldn't know the difference between a North Dakota farm boy and a ping pong champion in New York. And so it is in ALL schools of psychotherapy. Now I'll give you an illustration from every day life. I was returning from high school one day and a runaway horse with a bridle on sped past a group of us into a farmer's yard looking for a drink of water. The horse was perspiring heavily. And the farmer didn't recognize it so we cornered it. I hopped on the horse's back. Since it had a bridle on, I took hold of the tick rein and said, "Giddy-up." Headed for the highway. I knew the horse would turn in the right direction. *I* didn't know what the right direction was. And the horse trotted and galloped along. Now and then he would forget he was on the highway and start into a field. So I would pull on him a bit and call his attention to the fact the highway was where he was SUPPOSED to be. And finally, about four miles from where I had boarded him, he turned into a farm yard and the farmer said, "So THAT'S how that critter came back. Where did you find him?" I said, "About four miles from here." "How did you know you should come HERE?" I said, "I didn't know. The HORSE knew. All I did was keep his attention on the road." I think that's the way you do psychotherapy. . .

Over the course of that day and many subsequent days we discovered, learned, and changed. We discovered and learned about levels and forms of communication that we never knew about before, and gained new sensitivities about those with which we were already familiar. And in each of us Dr. Erickson planted seeds of change that continue to flower in our personal and professional lives. It is exciting to learn and grow. We hope that you will find the pages to come seeds that you can plant in your own personal and professional desert gardens.

ABOUT THE BOOK

We, the authors, are modelers of human communication. That is, we identify within communicational systems (intra or inter-personal) those patterns which are instrumental in producing the consistent outcomes of those systems. Richard Bandler, John Grinder, and Judith Delozier, for example, have described in their books, *Patterns of the Hypnotic Techniques of Milton H. Erickson, M.D., Volumes I & II*, many of the verbal and sensory system patterns Dr. Erickson uses in inducing altered states of consciousness. These patterns constitute, then, a *model* (map/functional description/technology) of how Erickson uses language and sensory systems to assist others in achieving trance states. What is significant about Bandler, Grinder and Delozier's work is that if you use those same models (technology) in your own hypnotic work they will make it possible for you to induce trance states in your clients in much the same way and with similar effect as was characteristic of Erickson's own inductions.[1]

For whatever reasons, a great deal of descriptive and modeling attention has been paid to Erickson's hypnotic work, and almost no such attention has been accorded his therapeutic work. Anyone who has had the priveledge of a teaching seminar with Erickson can note that most of the case studies that he describes do not involve the use of formal hypnotic inductions.[2] And, so, THIS is a book about the patterns of *therapeutic* intervention of Milton Erickson. Dr. Erickson has long been known for both his unique therapeutic approaches and his remarkable successes in assisting others to achieve happy, fulfilling, and productive lives. Anyone who has read accounts of Dr. Erickson's remarkable therapeutic interventions (such as are contained in Jay Haley's *Uncommon Therapy*) has surely been awed by this man's incredible versatility and effectiveness. Dr. Erickson's ability to create successful therapeutic environments within any problem context seems to be nothing less than magical . . . and it is. It is the magic of a consummate communicator. There is much to be learned from Milton Erickson. How to go about it?

In this volume we will be examining patterns we have identified in Dr. Erickson's creation, organization, and utilization of therapeutic interventions. It is our experience that much of the therapeutic magic that he is capable of producing can be learned by anyone willing to invest some time and effort in learning the patterns to be described throughout this book.[3] The patterns we offer you here are *descriptions* of what Erickson does. They are a way of talking about, a way of looking at, a way of grasping what he does. And what makes these patterns worth your interest is that they work—that is, if you learn and use them you will be able to reproduce in your own therapeutic work many of the seemingly magical outcomes that are characteristic of Erickson's work. We hope and assume that once you have mastered the patterns of interventions outlined here that they will drop out of your conscious experience to join the rest of your naturally occurring and organized behavior and intuitions.

A characteristic of written information is that it is sequential—the words follow one another and it is only over time as you read them that the patterns they describe coalesce into a comprehensive representation. The difficulty with this in relation to the task before us is that Erickson's astounding effectiveness in working with his clients is a result of the *simultaneous interaction* of many patterns within his behavior. The many patterns we will be describing in the chapters to come (as well as those found in the treatises of others) are presented individually, giving the impression that they are in themselves effective interventions, entities to be "applied" when needed. This sequential presentation is only for the purpose of clarity, however. The fact is that all of the patterns that we describe here are not only characteristic of Erickson's work at virtually every moment in time, but that these patterns are interrelated, their effectiveness directly dependent upon their interaction.

Anyone who has had the privilege of spending even a short time with Milton Erickson has surely come to appreciate the rich and important contribution of his voice tonality, pacing, and body movements to the overall meaning and impact of his communications. Indeed, those qualities are some of the most meaningful and impactful attributes of his communications. In the hope of preserving as much of those qualities as possible, we have chosen in this volume to use verbatim transcripts taken during our visits with Dr. Erickson so that he can describe his case studies to you in his own words. Punctuation, phrasing, and emphasis have been used in the transcripts to translate as accurately as possible some of the characteristics of the original tapes. No Boswell could match Erickson's own descriptions of his enterprise, and so through this device we hope you will discover in those stories and studies not only therapeutic techniques, but a man with a twinkle in his eye.

THE PHOENIX

Before this book was completed, Milton Erickson died, and his ashes are now atop Squaw Peak. And yet you will notice that throughout this book we persist in talking about him as though he is still alive. This is not a sign that our aberrations have finally surfaced and reality now slips through our fingers (and if it is so, we welcome it). It is instead a reflection of our certainty that much of what made Milton Erickson unique and important never died . . . never will. He spent his life parceling out little pieces of himself to any and all who would take them, and never held back a morsel, for he knew that for every piece he gave two more would grow in its place. And so it was and is. Milton Erickson is so thoroughly scattered about through each of us whom he touched, that the continuity of his existence goes on. And each time one of us delights in the intricacies of another human being, tries something new, looks hopefully into the future, or laughs at our personal and collective foibles, Milton Erickson, like the Phoenix, rises again from the ashes.

Now how do you do a hard piece of work? Bert and Lance planted a garden in Michigan for me, and I paid for the garden produce the same price I paid at the vegetable stand . . . That's how they got their spending money— they WORKED for it. I had a potato patch. Thirty rows —LONG rows—you know how potatoes are planted, they're planted in *hills* . . . one potato, one potato, one potato . . . and you hoe the dirt UP around the base of the plant, and the potato will form underground. Thirty long *rows,* and to HOE them is a *great big job.* How can you get two little boys to *hoe* a great big field? You have

them hoe row by row and the field is STILL as big . . .
Have them hoe a diagonal line, from here to *here,* and
hoe a diagonal line here and across and down the middle
and kept cutting that field down into little pieces, and
making more and more designs, and it's FUN to make
designs. They transferred hard work into *play.*

Footnotes

1. For a very much more complete description of modeling (as well as excellent examples of its use) the reader is referred to *Neurolinguisitic Programming, Volume I,* by Dilts, Grinder, Bandler, Cameron-Bandler, and Delozier; and to *The Structure of Magic, Volume I,* by Bandler and Grinder.

2. If you are familiar at all with Erickson's patterns of hypnotic communication (see Bandler and Grinder, 1975, and Grinder and Bandler, 1977) you will, of course, recognize that Erickson's communications are almost always hypnotically organized. However, his use of *formal* trance states, although useful and intriguing, is not nearly as ubiquitous in his work as is implied by the descriptive and analytical interest it has commanded. (If you have not been involved in one of Erickson's teaching seminars, see Zeig, 1980.)

3. That you can learn to reproduce in your own behavior the *technology* of Dr. Erickson's work is not to say that you will *become* Milton Erickson by virtue of that technology. The choices that you make when selecting the content to be employed by that technology will be your own, characteristic of you and your personal history, just as Erickson's choice of content is the unique result of his personal history. The anology is one of learning carpentry—a master cabinet maker can teach you to use woodworking tools and techniques as skillfuly as he does, but the pieces of furniture that you go on to make with those skills will be a function of your own aesthetics.

CHAPTER 2

Pygmalion

T here once lived on the island of Cyprus a fine sculptor, named Pygmalion, who had decided to devote himself entirely to his art because he could not find a woman to match his idea of beauty. Soon a very pure piece of white marble came into his studio and from it he sculpted a beautiful woman—a figure which embodied all that he considered beautiful. Pygmalion was so smitten with his own creation that he prayed to Aphrodite to help him find a woman that would match his sculpture's beauty. Aphrodite, however, realized that only the statue itself would answer for Pygmalion, and so she breathed into it the life that Pygmalion so fervently sought. Pygmalion called her Galatea and married her, his own creation.

Pygmalion is certainly not alone in his possession of standards and beliefs about what is or is not beautiful. Regardless of how they come into being, we all have personal beliefs about what constitutes beauty, intelligence, appropriate behavior, useful goals, and so on. None of us means, says, does or goes after just ANYTHING. There are always certain possibilities in the world which an individual will in some way delete from his or her experience (even the person who believes that "being open to everything" is important is deleting the possibility of being open only to certain things or being open to nothing). It is, of course, the differences in what we each hold as personal standards or beliefs that make each of us somehow unique.

There is another way in which we are all like Pygmalion. Sometimes intentionally, often unconsciously, we imbue the world around us with our own ideas about the way the world is, or should be. Any time you communicate with another person what you communicate will be an expression, a manifestation, of the beliefs that constitute your personal model of the world. And if, like Pygmalion, you are artful in your use of the communicational tools and skills you have at hand you might recreate in your conversational partner a belief or standard that matches your own. This happens when your trend-conscious friend announces the new chic and you proceed to clean out your closet, or when a therapist convinces you that a good cry will cure you and you proceed to let the tears flow.

In our experience, most psychotherapists are like Pygmalion in that they have, as individuals, learned certain ways of understanding the world of behavior and experience, and then, if they are artful, imbue their clients with those same understandings. For instance, Transactional Analysts teach their clients to think of their experiences as manifestations of parent, adult, or child states. There are certainly other possibilities for partitioning experience and behavior; what about infant, teenager, and senescent ego states, or hypo-reactive, reactive, and hyper-reactive states? A rational emotive therapist will teach you to organize and examine your beliefs against certain criteria of logic and rationality. These are examples of "institutionalized" sets of beliefs, values and perceptual distinctions. Similarly, but at the level of the individual, we have witnessed over and over again the phenomenon that a therapist who has discovered in his own experience happiness from always telling others what he wants, will then explicity or implicity attempt to install that same belief and accompanying behaviors in his clients. A therapist who, in his/her personal life, finds release from nagging problems through meditation will typically, when presented with a client who is nagged by problems, suggest the client try meditation. It is, of course, the function of a therapist to assist his or her client in altering or gaining a new belief, standard, or behavior. The purpose of these examples, however, is to highlight our observation that very often the kind of changes that a particular therapist will pursue with clients are those that are consistent with the *therapist's* model of the world (professional training and personal experiences) rather than being a function of, and in relation to, the *client's* model of the world. The point is that our private and professional beliefs/-standards/rules do not encompass what is possible, but instead LIMIT what is possible. And so, like Pygmalion, therapists can unintentionally produce clones of themselves through their clients. This is not in itself bad or wrong, but for its efficacy it is dependent upon the presuppositions that what is effective for one person can be effective for another, that problem situations that share a common name and experiential description are structurally isomorphic, and that the suggested solution is both acceptable to the individual and capable of being duplicated.

One thing that is so very remarkable about Milton Erickson is his consistent ability to succeed with clients of every kind of background and with every kind of problem. What makes it possible for Erickson to be so consistently successful is that the changes he makes in a client's beliefs or behavior are always in relation to the CLIENT'S model of the world. Erickson is not uniformly effective because he can hypnotize people—he is effective because he can use hypnosis in a way that fits his client's model of the world. Erickson is not successful because he knows the correct "treatment" for each particular kind of problem—he is successful because he uses the client's model of the world to guide the creation of an appropriate intervention. Naturally —invariably—you pursue therapy in a way that is consistent with your notions about what is the appropriate way to proceed. And just as naturally you ask questions, react to answers, and make suggestions that are all in accordance with what you believe to be appropriate, worthwhile, important, meaningful, and so on. For example, think of some issue (such as monogamy, honesty, death, astrology) about which you have at some time substantially changed your beliefs. If you compare your responses (the things you said, felt, and even your facial expressions) to that issue before and after you changed your beliefs you will probably discover that your responses *also* changed. That seems trivial, however it is important to take the sequence one step further and recognize that, unless intentionally controlled for, your behavior and communications within the context of therapy are just as much a function of your personal beliefs and, useful or not, will place certain constraints on the nature of your interaction with your client.

Milton Erickson is, of course, no exception in that he also holds certain beliefs and generalizations that inevitably, pervasively, guide his therapeutic interactions along certain paths. This book is, in fact, a presentation of those beliefs and generalizations that Milton H.

Erickson used to guide his therapeutic interactions with clients, and of those beliefs that he consistently instilled in those clients. This volume is not intended to be a description of the "right" way to do therapy, but is instead an accessible (that is, reproducible by you) description of those beliefs and generalizations about therapy and change that characterize Erickson.

What is to be learned from Milton Erickson is not so much a set of techniques but a new and useful way of looking at and grasping human behavior and its consequences, and of organizing therapeutic encounters. This includes such considerations as: who decides what changes are to be made, what should be the nature of the relationship between the client and the therapist, what is the function of insight, and what generalizations about life are useful and appropriate to have. We will be dealing with these questions from Erickson's viewpoint in this chapter. We think them worth including and worth your careful attention for two reasons. The first is that it has been our experience that by adopting as our own Erickson's criteria for psychotherapy, our ability to gracefully and rapidly achieve effective and lasting changes in our clients has become remarkable. The second is that (and it is true for anyone) it is our experience that Erickson's personal orientation towards life and his overall therapeutic techniques are intimately connected, such that if you adopt either one the other will naturally develop over time. We suggest, then, that you consider carefully the discussions in this chapter. They are relatively brief and not at all exhaustive explications of what may at first seem to be nonpivotal considerations, but their implications are far reaching. You may find that you will come to agree with us that, in fact, they are, more than any other considerations, responsible for shaping all of Erickson's therapeutic work. What follows (and, in fact, everything to be described in this volume) are some choices—Milton Erickson's choices —about how to organize one's perceptions and judgements of the world. These are not intended to replace your present criteria but are, *if* you find them useful, to be ADDED to what you now enjoy as your own repertoire of perceptions and understandings.

PALADINS OF CHANGE

Erickson considers it axiomatic that, by the time a client reaches his office, that person has already done everything that he consciously

KNOWS to do in order to change himself. There are a few professional clients who pit their frustrating skills against those of one therapist after another, but most individuals who walk into the offices of psychotherapists are there because they congruently need and want assistance in changing themselves. Invariably, the problems clients describe originated sometime in the dim or not-so-dim past. Problems that therapists hear about start in childhood, or in college, last year, or even some days ago, but never a few moments ago. Environmental unpredictability is sufficiently capricious to insure that life is forever punctuated by pitfalls, stumbling blocks, and brick walls, but for the most part people have the practical and existential coping skills they need in order to somehow deal with those exigencies. So it is reasonable to assume that many more people experience both minor and serious problems than those that seem to find their way to the offices of therapists. And (hopefully) it is also probable that even those who are receiving counseling never reveal to their therapists all of the various niggling problems with which they daily deal. The fact is that most people cope satisfactorily most of the time.

Ask any of your clients what they have done to try and solve their problems and they will tell you precisely what will not work in making the change they desire. Over and over again you will discover that people try everything that they KNOW to do to alleviate their problems, and when their personal skills prove ineffective they turn to friends, self-help books, therapists, and any other source of new information available. You as a therapist become a sought-after resource only when an individual discovers through his or her own unsuccessful efforts that he or she does not have, or is not able to properly use, the personal resources needed to satisfactorily handle the problem being faced. Very often clients enter therapy with either the conscious or unconscious orientation that they are there to be worked ON and that the therapist is to do that work. They have come up against a hurdle which they believe their personal resources are incapable of helping them scale, and like a man with a broken car and two left thumbs they are taking their problem to someone more skilled in the area than they are.

In view of the obvious lack in present behavior of needed coping skills in most clients (otherwise they would not be in your office), Erickson considers it the responsibility of the therapist to use his experience, knowledge, present information, and intuitions to determine just what kind of change will be most effective and appropriate for the individual before him. They may know that what they presently do isn't working and, perhaps, what they want to have as an outcome, but they do not usually know what they need in terms of a new experience or behavior in order to achieve that desired outcome. And as Erickson often points out, all they want is a change . . . any change. Accounts of Erickson's work with clients abound with examples of individuals being provided with experiences that seem to have little or no connection with their original request for help but which in the end proved thoroughly effective in achieving the changes being sought. An important corollary of Erickson's premise that his clients have already done what they know to do with respect to their problems is that an individual's inability to satisfactorily meet personal or societal expectations is usually not due to willful neglect, intentional maliciousness, or genetics, but is instead the result of insufficient or inappropriate learning experiences. Understanding people in this way renders those ubiquitous entities, BLAME and GUILT, irrelevant and, so, frees the therapist from intentionally or unintentionally condemning or pitying the things individual clients have done and from identifying family members as devils and angels.

Now patients that come to you, come to you because they don't *know* exactly WHY they come. They have problems, and if they knew what they WERE they wouldn't *have come.* And since they don't know what their problems REALLY are they can't tell *you.* They can only tell you a rather confused account of what they think. And you listen with YOUR background and you don't *know* what they are saying, but you better *know* that you don't know. And then you need to try to do SOMETHING that induces a *change* in the patient . . . any little change, because that patient wants a *change,* however small, and he will accept that AS a *change.* He won't stop to measure the EXTENT of that change. He will accept that as a change and then he will follow that change and the change will develop in accord with his own *needs* . . . It's much like rolling a snowball down a mountainside. It starts out a small snowball, but as it rolls down it gets larger and larger . . . and it becomes an avalanche that fits the shape of the mountain.

What kind of changes Erickson chooses to initiate in therapy will be dealt with in detail in Chapters IV and V. However, in regards to Erickson's personal orientation with respect to the selection of tasks and changes for clients it is appropriate to mention here that he admonishes therapists to not plan therapy, but to allow the events of each session and your unconscious mind to present you with the information and direction you need.[1]

> I always *trust* my unconscious. Now, too many psycho-
> therapists try to *plan* what thinking they will do instead
> of waiting to see what the stimulus they receive is and
> then letting their unconscious mind RESPOND to that
> stimulus . . . I don't attempt to structure my psychother-
> apy except in a vague, general way. And in that vague,
> general way the *patient* structures it. He structures it in
> accordance with his *own needs.* And the loose structure
> I create allows him to discover, bit by bit, some of the
> things he's repressed, doesn't know about himself. There
> are a lot of things we know that we don't *know* we know,
> but we need to KNOW that we know it . . . You trust your
> unconscious. It is a very delightful way of living, a very
> delightful way of accomplishing things. How many peo-
> ple plan to go to the Grand Canyon? They go from here
> to *there.* Now if *I* wanted to go to the Grand Canyon,
> I'd drive here, turn right, turn left . . . I'd eventually wind
> up in the Grand Canyon, I will have seen a lot of OTHER
> places. So whenever I went out driving on the desert on
> Sunday morning I'd turn right and left at random . . . I hit
> a LOT of places I didn't KNOW existed.

Erickson is making the point that it is inadvisable to generate PRECONCEPTIONS about the nature of your client's problems. His reliance on responding to the present rather than to a pre-set plan is one way in which Erickson adjusts himself to the requirements of his clients rather than try to fit his clients into a predetermined set of requirements that may be inappropriate or, by the time of the next session, already obsolete. Another way in which Erickson insures the appropriateness of his interventions is to consider the efficacy and personal and ecological impact of those interventions within the environment in which his *client* lives.

> The first consideration in dealing with patients, clients or subjects is to realize that each of them is an individual. There are no two people alike. No two people understand the same sentence, the same way. And so in dealing with people you try not to fit them into your concept of what they should be, you should try to discover what their concept of themselves happens to be.

Too often intentionally or unintentionally therapists attempt to inculcate their clients with a way of looking at and dealing with the world that has worked well for the therapist and others but which is, perhaps, clumsy and inappropriate with respect to the *client's* experience of the world. Also, therapists frequently initiate changes in a client which are incompatible with the environment in which that person lives. Erickson not only makes changes which are consistent with his client's normal milieu, but whenever possible he also utilizes his client's normal environment to effect the desired changes. Ultimately, people spend little time in counseling offices and must be able to operate appropriately in their everyday worlds. Using the naturally occurring events of the client's world provides Erickson's interventions with a predictability and naturalness of effect that has become a hallmark of his work. Numerous examples of Erickson's use of environments will be found in succeeding chapters, but as an example:

> Once while I was in Milwaukee, lecturing, William asked me, "My mother's sister lives in Milwaukee. She is independently wealthy, very religious, she doesn't like my mother and my mother doesn't like her. She has a housekeeper come in, a maid come in every day to do

the housework, the cooking, and she stays alone in that big house, goes to church, has no friends there. She just attends church and silently slips away. And she's been horribly depressed for nine months. I'm worried about her and I'd like you to stop in and do something for her. I'm the only relative she has that she likes and she can't stand me. So call on her and see what you can do." So, a depressed woman . . . I introduced myself and identified myself thoroughly . . . asked to be taken on a tour of that house. In looking around I saw she was a very wealthy woman living alone, idle, attending church but keeping to herself, and I went through the house room after room . . . and I saw three African violets and a potting pot with a leaf in it being sprouted as a new plant. So I knew what to do for her in the way of therapy. I told her, "I want you to buy every African violet plant in view for yourself . . . those are yours. I want you to buy a couple hundred potting pots for you to sprout new African violets, and you buy a couple hundred gift pots. As soon as the sprouts are well rooted, for every birth announcement you send an African violet; for every Christening; for every engagement; for every wedding; for every sickness; for every death; every Church bazaar." And one time she had two hundred African violets . . . and if you take care of two hundred African violets you've got a day's work cut out. And she became the African Violet Queen of Milwaukee with endless numbers of friends. Just that one little interview. I just pointed her nose in the right direction and said "Giddyup". And she did all the rest of the therapy. And that's the important thing about therapy . . . you find out the potentials that are possible for your patients and then you encourage your patient to undertake them and sooner or later he'll get all wrapped up in it.

It is obvious that Erickson is very much in charge of what transpires during therapy. He decides what his clients need in the way of new experiences, how they should go about obtaining those new learnings, and then directs them in doing so. Despite his active, directorial orientation towards therapeutic relationships it is also Erickson's belief that if one can assign responsibility for the work of changing that that responsibility—and credit—belongs to the client. The role of the therapist is to provide his client with the suitable conditions under which to learn, but it is within the client that changes actually occur and any changes that do occur do so as the result of the client's own efforts. This is an important distinction to make for it shifts clients from being passive recipients of help to being active agents in their own progress towards change.

You can't *compel* a person to quit smoking. I had a man come in and say, "I'm sixty-five years old, I smoke three packs of cigarettes a day, I really can't *afford* to spend money that way, but I *do,* I'm sick and *tired* of coughing the way I do every morning, every night, I don't sleep very well, and my food has no taste at *all.* And I think it's my smoking so I want to quit." At the end of the hour I said, "I'm sorry sir, but in this whole hour of interview you've given me NO evidence that you really *want* to quit smoking." He went home and told his wife, and she said, "You go back to that shrink and you tell him I know you better than HE does, and I *know* you want to quit smoking!" The man came back. I said, "You're wasting your time, but I'll spend another hour with you HOPING TO FIND evidence that you want to quit smoking." At the end of the hour I said, "The truth is that you *don't* want to quit smoking." He went home and told his wife, and she said, "I'll go WITH you to see that shrink." And she told me that I should put her husband in trance and *make* him quit smoking. So I told her privately, "You can FORCE a person to quit smoking by various aversion techniques, but the aversion techniques won't LAST very long. You MOTIVATE them to quit smoking and if they don't WANT to quit smoking, however good their motivation is, they'll resume smoking." She said, "My husband wants to quit smoking, you put him in a trance and you see to it he *does.*" I said, "I'll put him in trance and give him a VERY strong motivation to quit smoking." I put him in a trance and told him, "Smoke as much as you wish. *Every time* you light a cigarette you put the equivalent in cash in pennies and nickels in a glass bottle, and *every day* in pennies and nickels you put in the jar the price of three packs of cigarettes." Well during the first week he got interested in the accumulation of coins in that bottle, he quit smoking so he would have plenty of money to put in the milk bottle. The first week he was very excited . . . he had never been able to save money *before.* There was the bottle filling up, and he began to plan a vacation. The first week went very well, the second week was glorious, and the third week left them very excited about their coming vacation. And in the fourth week the man told his wife, "I ain't *used* to sleeping soundly all night. I ain't *used* to not coughing. I ain't *used* to having my food taste good. I'm going back to smoking." She was so infuriated she had to call me up and tell me what he had done wrong, to which he added, "I'm STILL trying to sell the goddamn lie that I *want* to quit smoking." I remember one woman who said, "I want you to make it *hard* for me to smoke." I said, "I can SUGGEST ways . . . it's up to you to *keep it hard.*" She said, "And I know what will be hard. I'm overweight. Have me keep my cigarettes in the basement, and my matches in the attic, and I can have only one cigarette at a time, and I have to go down to the basement to get it, and I have to go up into the attic to light it. That amount of exercise will reduce my weight." And she got SO interested in weight loss she quit smoking.

She had a new *goal,* so she accomplished TWO things.

At the Boston State Hospital I finished my lecture, a gray haired woman came up to me and said, "Do you remember me?" I said, "The question implies I should." She said, "You certainly *should* remember me. You published a paper on me." I said, "Well, that doesn't help me recall." And she said, "I think I can jog your memory easily. I'm a grandmother *now.* And Jim is still practicing internal medicine." I recalled then. In 1930, when I joined the staff at Worcester, I met a young female resident, a very intelligent woman . . . actually very BRILLIANT, very *capable.* And she had suddenly in the last six months become profoundly neurotic, lost weight, couldn't sleep, was anxious. She sought consultation with other psychiatrists. She said, "I don't know what I'm anxious about. I don't know why I don't sleep. But I'm in TROUBLE and I *know* it. I'm in a state of anxiety all of the time." She had sat in on some of my experiments in hypnotic work there and one day she came to me in June and said, "Dr. Erickson, I've got a neurosis and I don't know what it *is.* Will you come to my apartment this evening? And put me in a deep hypnotic trance, and have me go and lie down on the bed. And you tell me . . . now think it over in my unconscious mind, all about whatever my problem is. Give me at least an hour. Maybe it will take TWO hours, maybe more, *I* don't know. And you come in on the hour and ask me if I'm through, and I'll tell you." And finally, about 10:30, she said, "I'll be through in less than half an hour and when you come to awaken me tell me I don't have to remember . . . but just talk casually with me, and then just before you leave you say to me, 'I believe there is something you ought to *know.*" So about 11:00 she was talking to me, and looked at the clock and at her wrist watch . . . a strange man in her apartment at 11:00 at night, what business did I have THERE? And I said in the form of chit chat, "There is something you ought to *know.*" She flushed and said, "Dr. Erickson, get out of here!! GET OUT!! Leave go away right away NOW get out of here!!!" So I took my departure. At the end of June her residency was finished and she disappeared from sight. I didn't know what had happened to her. In late September she came into my office. "Dr. Erickson, I got married to a young doctor by the name of Jim. And this is my day off. We both work at North Hampton State Hospital. It is my day off so I was lying in bed, luxuriating in my happiness and wondering what I had ever done to DESERVE all the happiness I have. All of a sudden I remembered that day in June, that evening I told you to get out of the apartment, and I think I owe you an explanation." She said, "In the trance state a long manuscript unrolled and there was a pro side and a con side. I wrote down the pros and cons about marrying Jim. I come from a wealthy family and had all the advantages of wealth, travel, opera. Jim came from the other side of the tracks. He knew only hard work and I'm brighter than he. And so in the trance state I wrote all the pros in favor of marrying him. I wrote down all the cons. And then I started reading them. I crossed out this con and this pro —they cancelled each other. And I kept on cancelling pros and cons. I finally ended up with a lot of pros and no cons. And when you said, 'there is something you ought to know' I thought in my mind, "I'M going to marry Jim" and it bewildered me because I had dated Jim a few times . . . I liked him and Jim showed he liked me. But I had all the hesitations, and this morning I recalled that hypnotic experience so I drove from North Hampton to Worcester to tell you all about it." That was at Boston State Hospital and Jim was still practicing internal medicine. Now, that was just that ONE evening . . . a complete

alteration of her life and / didn't know what in the hell
I had done. Nor did SHE until September . . . she had
been married in July.

One manifestation of this point of view is that Erickson's efforts in therapy are usually directed towards getting his clients to do things *out in the world* that are intended to provide the needed experiences. We will talk in detail about what kinds of things Erickson has clients do and how he goes about getting them to do them in Chapter V, but for now we feel it important to point out one result of assigning clients active participation in making the changes they want. That is that in doing so they learn that they *are* capable of exercising control over their lives and of effecting changes they know they need to make. This seems to us an excellent investment in an individual's future. Such an orientation changes the tenor of therapy from "I, the therapist, am doing things to you to change you" to "I, the client, am doing things to change myself". Far too often therapists in the sincere desire to secure happiness and contentment for their clients inadvertently foster a dependent working relationship which tacitly accepts the necessity of professional therapeutic intervention for making changes. Consequently, many people come out of therapy pleased with the changes they have made AND the knowledge that they needed a therapist's help to do it. Too often this experience becomes generalized into the rule: "If I am encountering difficulties in my life, go to a therapist". Many will argue that there is nothing wrong with such a rule. Erickson, however, is not only interested in alleviating presenting problems but is also interested in assisting his clients in becoming autonomous individuals, with access to, and capable of, using all of their personal resources so that he or she can do his own therapy when needed. As therapists and trainers of therapists it is our observation that modern therapies still emphasize to excess the remedial aspects of therapy (that is, the amelioration of a particular problem or symptom) and devote too little attention to creating generative individuals, people capable of creating for themselves those experiences they need or want.

ORPHEUS

> About a year ago I had a woman write to me, "I've been
> in psychoanalysis actively being analyzed for *thirty years.*
> I'm now completing FOUR years of Transactional Analy-
> sis and when I finish I'd like to be your patient" . . . I told
> her my resources were limited.

Erickson does not believe that conscious insight into one's problems
is a necessary prerequisite for achieving meaningful changes and, in
fact, is usually quite useless. To begin with, unearthing the roots of a
problem often requires a long stretch of digging, as anyone undergoing
psychoanalysis knows. This painstaking bringing-to-light of the past
would be justified if such knowledge brought about the desired changes.
It is our experience, however, that the mere knowledge of the origin of
an emotional problem rarely results in a "cure". It may provide useful
information for the therapist, and perhaps temporary relief through
catharsis, but in and of itself does little more than satisfy a client's
curiosity. When in our private practice clients congruently request a
conscious understanding of the historical forces underlying their present difficulties we sometimes explore the question with them until they
are satisfied. And when we ask them if now knowing "why" they do
what they do changes anything, the inevitable answer is, "No, not
really." There is, then, serious question as to whether insight into one's
problems is useful or necessary in correcting them. Furthermore,
achieving insight can be very time consuming. Erickson has demonstrated in his work over and over again that insight is not at all a
necessary prerequisite or concomitant of growth and change. For
example:

> How much therapy does a person *need?* First year I joined
> the faculty at Wayne State Medical School the Dean
> called me in the first day and said, "Erickson, there is a
> senior student . . . when he was a sophomore he lost his leg
> in an automobile accident. He wears an artificial leg.
> Before he lost his leg he was an outgoing, sociable person-
> ality . . . always friendly, outgoing, a hail-fellow well met.
> With the fitting of his artificial leg he became withdrawn,

lost all of his friends, unresponsive." Then the Dean said, "And please don't say the word 'leg' in his presence. He overreacts to it." And I said, "All right, I'll take care of that." I waited 'til the students got acquainted with me. It took about three weeks. And then I selected Jerry, Tom and Joe. I told them, "You spread the word that I'm going to pull one of my, uh, classical pranks. And you don't know what it IS. Just spread the rumor that Erickson is up to something." And the next Monday morning, "Jerry, you go to the fourth floor and hold the elevator up there. And Tom you stand at the head of the stairwell and look down on the ground floor. And Joe you be on the ground floor pressing the elevator button and cussing because the janitor is keeping the elevator up so he could get his mops and pails down." The rumor having been spread, of course EVERYBODY was there at 7:30 . . . even as *I* was. And I walked in, acted surprised to see them all at 7:30. We stated a few words of chit chat about the weather, I said, "Why don't you punch the elevator button Joe?" Joe said, "That damn janitor is keeping it up on the fourth floor I suspect. He is worried about getting his mops and pails down." Still further chit chat, began to suggest to Joe he push the elevator button. And at about five minutes to eight the lights lit up on the second floor. I turned to this hyper-sensitive student with an artificial leg off in one corner and I said, "Let's us cripples hobble up *stairs* and leave the able-bodied to wait for the elevator." So us cripples started hobbling upstairs. Tom saw us, signaled Jerry, Jerry released the elevator, the rest of the class came up on the elevator. At the end of the hour that withdrawn student had resumed his social attitude. All I had done was *alter the way he* LOOKED at things. The way he SAW himself. I lifted him out of the status of a cripple and I identified him with a professor who ALSO had a limp. That gave him a new status, and so for the rest of the year he really enjoyed his stay in medical school. And it is a very simple thing. How many therapists would have gone into the family history, history of the accident, the adjustments he made, and so on. And that he SHOULD make. All *I* did was yank him out of his unfortunate situation and drop him into a new situation that he COULD handle. And HE did all the rest of his therapy, all by himself.

Now that's short therapy. It's therapy without insight. This devoted probing into the past and mulling it over and over and over endlessly . . . And there is nothing you can change about the past. You live tomorrow, next week, next month, hopefully next year and so you go ahead wondering what is round the next corner. And enjoy life as you go along.

GENERATIVE GENERALIZATIONS

Like everyone else, Milton Erickson had his own criteria about what kinds of lessons are important for people to learn so that they can enjoy happy and productive lives. The three that seem to permeate his work most often are learning to be flexible, to have a sense of humor about oneself and the world, and to look to the future. These highly valued criteria are rarely the explicit goal of his therapeutic interventions. Nevertheless, Erickson almost always weaves into his work with clients experiences which at least peripherally include new learnings about personal flexibility, humor, and orientating towards the future, and, in any case, these generalizations characterize all of Erickson's communications and interactions. Erickson's efforts towards reorientating his clients in regards to these abilities make it possible for whatever changes he effects to have a continuing impact on his clients. Again, as we pointed out in a previous section, one of Erickson's goals within the therapeutic relationship is to tap and make available those generative resources his clients need in order to become self-sufficient individuals. This frequently means not only correcting the presenting problem but providing those learnings needed for successful future coping as well.

Flexibility

> I can remember walking to the lake in the 1930's accompanied by another psychiatrist who had always lived in the city. There were a lot of *trees* around the lake. I walked through very *comfortably,* and he disgustedly, again and again, angrily commented on the branches of the trees, *striking him* unexpectedly, knocking his glasses off. So I had to tell him, "You *learn* how to walk through underbrush and trees, it's different than walking on bare land and bare sidewalks. You balance your BODY differently . . . and you automatically respond to a branch out of the corner of your eye without noticing it and you *alter* your body movements so that the branch will not impede your movements."

One way of describing your client's problems is in terms of flexibility vs. lack of flexibility. By "flexibility" we are referring to an individual's ability to regard a situation from different points of view and/or the ability to *respond to various situations in different and appropriate ways.* A client who tells you, "Every time I ask a girl out on a date I get so nervous that I can't talk!" is telling you that he is inflexible in his behavior within the context of "dating". That is, each time he is faced with a "dating" situation he invariably (inflexibly) responds by becoming nervous and mute. Since there are some occasions for which being mute is appropriate (during a sermon, for example) what this person needs is the *flexibility* of behavior to be able to be quiet in church, walk out of church, up to a prospective date and then be able to converse freely. It is Erickson's contention that the more choices (flexibility, variety) you have available in your own behavior the more likely it is that you will be able to successfully accommodate yourself to the vagaries of daily life. As a therapist this is, perhaps, even more important since what is demanded of you daily is that you somehow adjust yourself to understanding and working with one unique individual after another. We particularly want you to keep in mind the notion of flexibility as you read the case histories contained in this volume, for in all of them (as throughout all his work) Erickson demonstrates what is perhaps the most immediately striking characteristic of his work—his unprecedented ability to adjust his own behavior and communications to achieve whatever rapport and whatever end he feels appropriate and useful for the individual before him. And, often the "end" that his efforts are directed towards is that of nurturing in his *client* the ability to be flexible.

> And we ALL have our own rigidities without knowing it. I recall eating breakfast in a hotel in Chicago with a colleague who watched me eat my toast in ABSOLUTE *horror*. I could see the horror in his face. I didn't know what it meant . . . the TOAST was good! Finally he said, "What is the *matter* with you, haven't you got any *table manners* of ANY sort?" I said, "Why do you ask?" "You buttered that toast, broke it in two, and now you are eating *half* of it." I said, "That's right . . . it tastes very good." He said, "The PROPER way is you CUT your slice of toast in *four parts* and you pick each up separately and eat it." I asked him why and he said, "because that's the *only* WAY to eat toast!" So the next morning I ate my toast by the WHOLE toast without breaking it in half. He finally *learned* to eat toast *comfortably*.

Humor

> You need to teach patients to LAUGH off their griefs and to enjoy their *pleasures*. I had an alcoholic woman who came to me for therapy . . . and she was telling me the troubles she was having with her college-aged daughter. She said, "I've had trouble with her ever since she went riding in our . . ." what do you call that car that doesn't have a top? . . . a convertible. She was riding along . . . "we were having a happy time and a bird flying overhead happened to make a deposit just when she was *yawning*. And she's been SO ashamed with herself ever since. She just can't seem to face life at all. And my alcoholism doesn't help her." I said, "Well, tell me a few

MORE things about your daughter." "She's really a very nice girl, but she's awfully neurotic on that one subject." "Does she ever have a sense of humor?" The mother said, "Yes, but not since then." She had developed a lot of food avoidances that made her life very miserable. I asked the mother, "You said she has a good sense of humor but she hasn't USED it for a few years. Well you must have a lot of humor dammed up behind that capable person. So do you mind if I do a little therapy long distance?" The mother said, "No, I don't mind." So I mailed the girl a postcard from Philadelphia advising her about the *perils of yawning* while riding in a convertible. The girl got that card and said, "Who is that man and how did he EVER find out about it? I know *I never told him.* Did YOU tell him?!!" She said, "What's his name?" The girl said, "It's signed M. H. Erickson." And mother said, "I've never BEEN to Philadelphia. I don't know of anybody who lives in Philadelphia by THAT name. Isn't it rather a funny thing?" The girl burst into laughter and said, "It certainly *is.*" And she laughed, oh, uproariously for quite some time. And resumed normal living. It was just friendly advice.

Although many of the things that happen to people and that people themselves do are not obviously or inherently humorous, humor can be found in almost anything. Professional comedians know this and are able to make us laugh about divorce, unemployment, phobias, poverty, insecurity, and even death. Well-placed humor is somehow capable of taking the sting out of a pain, of making new or frightening topics more acceptable, and of taking the gravity out of a situation so that it no longer excessively weighs one down. Erickson understands the usefulness of humor in coping with setbacks and unpleasant surprises, and he not only uses his own infectious sense of humor effectively but he is able by example and experiences to instill in his clients a similarly lighthearted perspective on the comings and goings of human beings.

The fundamental thing that people should *learn* is that there should be NO place in their lives for hurt feelings. When you get hurt feelings *run,* don't walk but *run,* to the nearest garbage can and get *rid* of them and you'll live much more happily. Anyone that wants to INSULT you . . . it's all right. I'm thinking of the story of the Irishman and the Jewish rabbi. The Irishman *hated* Jews. He met the rabbi one morning . . . proceeded to vilify the rabbi, calling him every insulting name he could. When Pat ran out of insults the rabbi said gently, "Pat, when someone gives you a present and you don't want it, what do you do? Do you take it?" Pat said, "I sure don't!" The rabbi said, "You've offered me a present of insults, I don't want it, so keep it for yourself."

The Future

Then there was John. John met everybody who came on the ward. He pestered the nurses explaining, "I'm locked up here for no reason at all. I don't belong here." So I instructed the entire ward personnel every-time he says "I don't belong here," I said, "reply to him simply 'But you *are* here'." After about six months of always getting that same reply John said, "I KNOW I'M HERE!!" The ward personnel reported this to me and I went to him and he said, "I don't belong here", and I said, "But you are here." He said, "I know I'm here." I said, "That's right you are here. Now that you are here what do you want to do about *LEAVING* here?" Within nine months he was discharged, got a job as a manual laborer and started putting his sister through college and contributing to the support of the family. Having no psychotherapy other than, "You ARE here." Forcing a patient to recognize where they are at and meeting them there and then bridging the gap to the future is a very important thing.

Freud's most enduring legacy is the notion that the key to present problems lies buried in one's past. That the antecedents of one's problems are to be found in one's past is undeniably true. That the antecedents of a problem and the key to its solution are one and the same thing is much less tenable. As we discussed in a previous section, knowing "why" someone does what he does is not a prerequisite for assisting him in changing. Furthermore, regardless of when or where the key comes from, if and when it finally gets turned it will be turned *now* or in the *future*—not in the past. Clients usually enter a counselor's office lugging behind them a history of examination and reexamination of the nature and origins of their problems. This, Erickson feels, is a waste of valuable time and much of his therapeutic work is either implicitly or explicitly directed at reorientating his clients towards looking ahead rather than behind.

In 1933 a fellow psychiatrist and I were sitting talking. He *was* an excellent psychiatrist. He handled his patients in a very objective fashion, a *very* competent man professionally but PERSONALLY he was extremely neurotic. And in 1933 he said he was going to resign, and go into psychoanalysis. I told him, "Bob, why are you going into psychoanalysis?" He said, "Well, I want to get over my fear of women. I want to marry, have a home and children." I said, "Bob, if you're not over your fear of women by 1940, *forget* therapy." In 1965 his mother *died,* and he was still in psychoanalysis. Several of his analysts had died, and he was STILL in therapy. His mother died in her 90's, and the mother had lived with an elderly woman as a companion. Now after the mother's death there was no place for that elderly woman to go, so Bob MARRIED her. She was fifteen years older than he. They bought a home, a very much in disrepair summer cottage in Vermont. They spent TWO summers working hard to get that summer cabin suitable for occupancy during the summer months and lived in a small apartment in Boston . . . Recently Bob died. Now he had been left independently wealthy by his father. His life long ambition was to go to

Scotland. He got as far as Massachusetts and Windsor, Canada—that was as close as he got to Scotland. All that psychoanalysis, from '33 to past 1965 'til he *died.* And he married a woman fifteen years his SENIOR. She was 80 when he was 67—that couldn't really be called a marriage. He didn't really have a wife. She certainly was not fit to have children and he didn't have a home—he only had a small apartment in Boston. And yet, when he worked for the hospital he was a very competent psychiatrist so far as his PATIENTS were concerned. And so many psychoanalyzed patients I see have spent *years* in the futile examination of their past and I say, let's *forget* the past and look forward to the future . . . and above all put humor in whatever you do!

Footnotes

1. Remember that Erickson's "unconscious mind" (that is, his non-conscious computations) is already organized with respect to the patterns we and others have modeled. In order for you or anyone else to be able to "unconsciously" produce Ericksonian therapeutic interactions and interventions you must first train yourself to reproduce his computational patterns. Once those patterns have been learned (that is, they are appropriately contextualized and you are systematic in using them), you will be free to depend upon your mind to make those computations even when you are "unconscious" of the process.

CHAPTER 3

Avatar

Rapport and the Pacing of Experience

The first consideration in dealing with patients, clients, or subjects is to realize that each of them is an individual. There are no two people alike. No two people understand the same sentence the same way. And so in dealing with people you try not to fit them into your concept of what they should be . . . you try to discover what their concept of themselves happens to be.

Now Betty thinks in a straight line, and I think all over the place. Now, I purchased the boys their bicycles. I warned them that they should keep the pressure up in their tires, I gave them a pressure gauge and told them that they should keep it on the intercom. Our kitchen was in the basement, we lived on the second floor. Got an intercom so Betty could hear the babies crying. One evening I came home from the office, there on the kitchen table was the pressure gauge. I said, "Oh oh, the boys got careless. I'll have to punish them for that. I'll hide the pressure gauge." I said, "I know, I'll drop it in the garbage pail." Betty said, "That'll be the FIRST place that Bert looks." I said, "That's probably right. I'll hide it in that quart measure up on that shelf." She says, "That will be the second place he looks!" I said, "All right, I'll hide it the way YOU would hide it." The boys came in the kitchen. I said, "How's the air pressure in your tires?" They said, "UH OH—pressure gauge!" I said, "That's right. I hid it." Bert said, "Oh, it'll be in the garbage pail." Betty said, "I told Dad that's the first place you would look." Bert said, "Oh, how about the quart measure?" "I told Dad that was the second place you would look. So he hid it the way *I* would hide it." Bert said, "Oh", and leaned against the doorway, and said, "I'll let Lance find it." Lance wandered from the kitchen to the breakfast room, back and forth. He always paused by the radio on the opposite side of the room by the intercom. He looked under it, on top of it, behind it. Didn't find it. He went back and forth, looking everywhere, always pausing at the radio. About the third time, Bert said, "The tire gauge is in the radio." Walked over and picked up the radio, reached inside, and hauled it out. The radio and intercom are forms of communication and Betty thinks in a straight line. And I think every therapist ought to become acquainted with straight line thinking, and, oh . . . what do you call it? . . . scattered thinking!!

A basic requirement for successful therapy is trust. Most individuals do not enter into therapy lightly. Rather it is usually an important and momentous step accompanied by frets about appearing a failure, foolish, awful, or "naked" before another person. Professional confidentiality is, of course, an obvious and necessary first step in providing an atmosphere in which people can feel free to speak of their problems, but in and of itself it is not sufficient to ensure access to an effective therapeutic relationship. Before an individual seeking help feels safe in revealing necessary information and becomes receptive to new ideas he must first discover his therapist to be a trustworthy person who is capable of both understanding and accepting the client and his problem situation. This ability of a therapist and client to trustingly and comprehensively communicate with one another is what we refer to as "rapport". As we shall see in the sections to follow, rapport is neither the ability to be sympathetic nor does it mean being liked by one's client (although sympathy and pleasant interactions are often erroneously taken as evidence of being in rapport), but is the ability to symmetrically respond to another person's model of the world. Rapport is often cited as an essential ingredient to a successful therapeutic relationship, but *how* to go about establishing rapport is rarely described.

Now how DOES one create that seemingly intangible experience of trust? In general the attitude has been, "either it's there or it isn't." Consequently many therapists turn clients away, believing their paralyzing lack of rapport with that particular client to be an inherent function of a clash of characters. Because so little has been done to explicate and utilize those interactional elements which create rapport within the therapeutic relationship, much valuable time has been wasted by clients trying one therapist after another, resisting each in turn, until he or she comes upon one that that individual experiences as being trustworthy and perceptive. It is no doubt true that the experience of rapport between a client and therapist can result from the fortuitous conjunction of many subtle personality characteristics, but it is also true that there are some specific patterns of communication which create and foster rapport, and which can be effectively used by any therapist to secure a therapeutic relationship with any client.

One of the most powerful of these rapport-building patterns with which we are familiar is that of matching the client's characteristic use of *predicates* (words that specify action and relationships—verbs and their modifiers). Most individuals tend to depend upon one or another of their sensory systems (visual, auditory or kinaesthetic) for most of their *conscious* representations of ongoing experience. This specialization will be reflected in an individual's choice of predicates such that people who are highly visual (in terms of the sensory modality most often utilized for consciousness) will be heard to use words like "I *see*", "new *perspective*", and "that's *clear*" as their way of painting for you a picture of the particular experience they are focusing on at that moment. Correspondingly, those who are highly kinaesthetic will be heard to use words such as "I *grasped* the idea", "it's a *stumbling* block", and "let's *smooth* things out", when handing you descriptions of the many warm and chilling experiences they have wrenched from memory. And for still others an experience may "*ring* a bell", be "*screaming* for attention" or "in *harmony* with one's needs" when intoned by an auditory person giving voice to discordant passages in their lives. If the therapist matches his or her own predicates (visual, auditory, kinaesthetic) to those the client uses most often, the consistent result is that the client experiences the therapist as someone who (literally) speaks his or her language, understands and is *understandable,* and is therefore trustworthy. Familiar to many will be Virginia Satir as an example of a therapist who intuitively and exquisitely uses the matching of predicates in her work to quickly establish close rapport with each member of a family.[1] Erickson also utilizes predicates for the purposes of rapport and intervention throughout his work, the most evident examples being found in transcripts of his hypnotic inductions.[2]

Another means of establishing rapport (of which Erickson is a master) is that of mirroring the client's analogical behavior. By "analogue" we are referring to an individual's breathing rate, pulse, temperature, body posture, muscle tonus, facial expression, gross body movements, voice tonality, and intonation patterns (that is, everything other than the words being used). The effect of mirroring is that your behavior becomes so closely identified with that of the client's that you become for him an unconscious and accurate source of feedback as to what he is doing. At the most fundamental level mirroring involves directly copying some or all of the analogical behavior of the person before you. So, if your client talks with a high pitched voice and is fidgety, you match the behavior by raising your own tonality and by squirming in your chair. A more sophisticated level of mirroring is called "cross-over mirroring", and is the level at which Erickson usually operates. In cross-over mirroring you copy the analogical behavior you wish to mirror using a part of the body or an output system that is different from that being used by your client. For example, you could mirror the nervous bobbing of your client's foot by bobbing your head at the same tempo *or* by causing the pitch or loudness of your voice to rhythmically raise and lower to the tempo of the client's foot. Using his tremendous ability to notice breathing patterns, pulse rates, skin color changes, minute muscle tone changes, and so on, Erickson uses cross-over mirroring to quickly adapt his own tonality and body movements to those of his clients. Accordingly, Erickson may time the tempo of his voice to match his client's pulse rate, while the movements of his body correspond to changes in the client's breathing rate. The possibilities for the utilization of analogical mirroring to create rapport are limitless, and such utilization is one of the most important skills we teach participants in our training seminars.

There is another level at which Erickson establishes rapport which seems to us to inevitably constitute an important part of this, his first step in assisting others in changing. That is, he *demonstrates* to his clients, either by word or deed, that he understands them (their model of the world) and their problems. This demonstration of understanding (ie. *comprehension* rather than commiseration) becomes crucial for it is the foundation upon which are built the interventions which are to follow. As a consequence of this demonstration the client *knows* that the new learnings Erickson offers come from someone who understands the context in which they are to be utilized (that is, the client's world and situation). This is an important characteristic of Erickson's therapeutic work and is a natural consequence of his belief in the uniqueness of each individual.

Each individual who walks into your office brings with him a model of the world which is, as Erickson says, "as unique as his thumbprint". We not only start life with our own unique sets of genes, but thereafter no two of us grow up exposed to exactly the same experiences. Whether conscious of them or not, each individual has his own history of unique experiences and has organized those experiences into an equally unique set of judgements about the nature of the world and a set of rules to live by. And since one's behavior will be largely a function of those rules and generalizations, a person's behavior must be understood, and will only make sense, in relation to his or her own view of the world and the context in which that view is operating.

> It reminds me of a time in Florida. Mrs. Erickson and I entered a restaurant, took a seat in a booth. A young couple came in with an eighteen month old child . . . our waitress got a high chair and tried to butter up that eighteen month old baby and he turned his face down. And the parents said knowingly, "Oh baby is *very* shy, *very* timid, won't even look at strangers." The meal was served to the parents . . . I know what babies do. Pretty soon the baby started to look around. He looked in my direction and I ducked, and very quickly I ducked again. Pretty soon the baby and I were having a nice game of peek-a-boo. We lingered, and when the parents left the

baby waved bye-bye to me. The parents nearly fell over.
But you meet the patient at the *patient's* level.

What is obviously useful about your client's personal model of the
world is that since it is the set of filters and rules that makes up and
directs that person's experience and behavior, your client will have to,
naturally, respond to any utilization of that model. A most conspicu-
ous feature of Erickson's therapeutic approach is that he alters his *own*
model of the world to match that of his client. He accepts the clients'
world model rather than try to convince or force them to accept his,
and in doing so demonstrates to his client that they are in harmony
regarding an understanding of the nature of that person's situation.
One advantage of this orientation is that resistance is rarely a problem
in therapy simply because it is never created. Too often a therapist
takes the beliefs and behaviors of his client and tries directly or indirectly to convince that person that they are incorrect or inappropriate. The usual response on the part of the client is some form of overt
or covert resistance, not only to the new idea but to the well-meant
suggestions which follow.

I let the patient in talking to me give me clues. A defiant
child, one of my children, told me, "You can't make me
put this book in the bookcase." I told him I was sure I
couldn't MAKE him, and that I couldn't even keep him
from moving that book an *inch*. He showed me—he
could move it TWO inches, THREE inches. He
COULDN'T move it over near that chair. He showed me.
That chair, this chair. And he put the book in the bookcase. And you accept the patient's denial, their resistance, and USE it. I'll give you an example of that. A man
and his wife came in, married for seven years, and they
wanted me to settle their *quarrel*. He wanted to go on
vacation to California and Wyoming. She wanted to go
on vacation to North Dakota. She said angrily, "For seven
YEARS I've gone to California and Wyoming . . . same old
places, same old thing. This year I want my vacation
somewhat DIFFERENT." He said, "California and Wyo-

ming is good enough for me, and it is good enough for you." I said, "Well, if your wife thinks North Dakota is good enough for her, let her discover that maybe it ISN'T." So he obligingly agreed to go on vacation by himself . . . while she went to North Dakota. And one night at 2 A.M. I got a call from Wyoming. He said, "Did you send me on vacation separately so I'd get a divorce from my wife!?" I said, "We only discussed vacations." He said, "Oh", hung up, so did I. The next night at 1 A.M. I got a phone call from North Dakota saying, "Did you send me to North Dakota so I'd think about getting a divorce from my husband!?" I said, "No. We only discussed that you might like to GO to North Dakota." When they got back they got a divorce. Why should I enter into that acrimonious battle of should we get a divorce or should we not? Is he being fair? Is she being fair? They arrived at their decision independently. They punished me for it by calling at one and two a.m. Certainly *I* hadn't discussed divorce with them, why should I? The wife had gone along with the husband to the same old place for seven years and *hates* it all the time. It's not a vacation. She *hates* every minute of it. She's not getting much out of her marriage. And he's undoubtedly trying to PUNISH her into getting rid of him. But *I* wouldn't tell them that. I just advised separate vacations. They did all the rest of the therapy.

A year after the divorce the wife called me up, she said she wanted an appointment with me. I gave her one. She brought in her boyfriend, introduced him, and said, "I want you to talk to him. And I want you to tell us both what you think of EACH of us . . . and what you think of each of us in relation to the other." So I conversed with him . . . with her . . . found they had a community of interest, a similar sense of humor, a similar pattern of social living. So I told them, "You both seem to be very

nice people. You ought to be good friends, and maybe in
time you'll discover something *more.*" And that placed
them under NO obligation to commit themselves. It *did*
put them under obligation to discover something more.

Instead of attempting to directly change the world model which is
creating the unwanted situation, *Erickson uses the client's existing
world model to change the unwanted situation.* In telling the boy what
he *couldn't* do, Erickson was utilizing the polarity response that was
a characteristic of the boy's model of the world. Similarly, utilizing the
husband's wish to convince his wife of her error, Erickson's suggestion
of separate vacations became a way of vindicating the husband's asser-
tions. In both cases his clients had to respond in the way Erickson
intended for, after all, he was using *their* rules, their characteristic
ways of making sense. We cannot emphasize this point enough. The
most efficient, effective, and graceful way of leading an individual
towards any change is to utilize *their* model of the world to get them
where they want to go.

Notice that we are not here talking about determining "why" a
person operates out of the particular world model that he or she does,
nor are we talking about changing that model. What we are interested
in is the *utilization* of that model as a way of establishing rapport.
Most of an individual's generalizations about experience (their world
model) represent important coping strategies learned out of *necessity,*
usually reinforced through subsequent experience, and so, at the conscious or unconscious level are understandably guarded as tried-and-
true friends by their owner. Instead of challenging these generalizations Erickson in effect says, "Well, since they are so reliable in their
functioning and compelling in their impact, how can they be *used* to
point my client in the direction he wants to go?"

In order to provide you with a thorough sense of just how many
possibilities there are for matching your client's model of the world,
we have (somewhat arbitrarily) divided those possibilities into the
areas of "content," "behavior," and "culture." Other distinctions with
respect to model-matching can certainly be made (predicate matching, for example), but the three we use here should give you an idea
both of the range possible as well as assist you in identifying those
forms of model-matching that are characteristic of virtually all of
Erickson's work.

Content Rapport

Every person believes certain things to be true (descriptive, charac-teristic, etc.) about him or herself and the world and will often state those beliefs to you directly. For example: "I'm the kind of person who likes meeting people," "Most people think I'm smart," "I'm too short," "I'm a smoker," "I'm Jesus Christ". However, personal beliefs about the world and oneself are not always so explicitly stated as in the above examples, but instead are implicit in the communication. For example, we can infer that a person who asks his spouse, "How late should I stay up tonight?", believes that it is important to consult her, believes that she has useful information about him, and believes that there exists for him optimum times to remain awake or asleep. The point is that whenever an individual communicates with you, the content of that communication will be based on, and indicative of, certain beliefs within that person's model of the world.

Often what a person believes to be true about himself does not match what others see in him. The mother-in-law who makes daily visits to her children's home may think that her attentions character-ize her as a "caring person", while in fact her children consider her a "meddler". Of course, from mom's perspective she is right, and from the kid's perspective THEY are right. Many therapists either know-ingly or unknowingly take sides when faced with such experiential discrepencies and then attempt to persuade the person whose percep-tions have strayed from "reality" to match those selected by the therapist.

If (using our example from above) you tell the mother-in-law that she is not being "caring" but is actually "meddling" she is faced with two alternatives for making sense out of your communication, one of which is destructive of rapport, the other destructive of the therapeu-tic relationship: (1) If she denies your perception of the situation and holds to her belief that she is "caring" then she may mistrust you as someone whose perceptions are faulty and perhaps insulting. Why seek help from someone who does not understand you? (2) If she denies her own perceptions, accepting yours that she is a busybody, then she may mistrust her own ability to have accurate perceptions about herself and, so, become either wary of opening any further the lid to a possible Pandora's box and/or dependent upon others for tests of her own reality. As individuals dedicated to the nurturance of strong, self-reliant and growing human beings we can't imagine any

therapist finding either of these consequences therapeutically attractive. Confronting someone with how their model of the world is "not
so" or "bad" is destructive of client-therapist trust and/or destructive
of the client's trust of himself.

> There was one patient who said he was Jesus Christ. He
> was very paranoid and yet he was harmless and had
> ground privileges. And Worcester tried to use patients
> with ground privileges at useful tasks. And the Psychol-
> ogy Laboratory wanted a handyman. And here was this
> patient, wrapped up in a sheet, walking around commun-
> ing with God . . . very polite and courteous. And so I was
> told to do something with him. I told him how desirable
> it was for the doctors to play tennis in the recreation hour.
> They were using muscles and skills and abilities that God
> had endowed them with. And it was very imperative that
> the tennis grounds be kept in good shape . . . dirt court.
> And we wandered down to the tennis court. We made
> a lot of comments about the trees that God had made, the
> beautiful grass, the creations of the earth itself, and then
> I noticed that there were some rough spots on that dirt
> court and I told him I was sure that God didn't want those
> rough spots there and could he in some way succeed in
> having the tennis ground leveled carefully and smoothed
> out? He said he certainly would TRY, he was there to
> serve Mankind. So I left him. He was an excellent tennis
> court grounds keeper. As for the Psychology Laboratory,
> they wanted some bookcases built. I happened to men-
> tion Jesus was a carpenter. So he built the book cases. He
> became a handyman around the Psychology Laboratory.

Instead of attempting to directly alter his clients' beliefs, Erickson
demonstrates through the content of his own communications to
them that he understands and accepts their model of the world as
being valid. In this way Erickson nurtures in his clients the confidence
that he is a person who understands and can therefore be trusted. In

the above transcript, for instance, Erickson *demonstrated* to his patient that he accepted and understood the man's model of the world (that is, that he is Jesus) by talking about God and His handiwork, the patient's role as the Son of God, and the patient's well-known vocation as a carpenter. THEN Erickson goes on to utilize the implications of that world model (that is, that the man is the servant of Mankind and a carpenter) as the basis of altering his behavior. Similarly, rather than telling the mother-in-law of our other example that she is being a busybody, thereby jeopardizing rapport, you could praise her sincere concern and then go on to consider all of the ways there are to be attentive and concerned (such as giving people the chance to make mistakes so that you can REALLY help them). People seem to cling much more tenaciously to their beliefs than to the behaviors connected with those beliefs. Certainly as many people have been killed in the name of "peace" as in the name of "hate", for example. It seems, then, that your clients will be much more amenable to engaging in new behaviors when your mirroring of the content of their model of the world reassures them that you share it, and are preserving that model through your interventions. In this next case Erickson again simply accepts the content of the client's beliefs regarding his situation and then demonstrates that acceptance in the content of his own communications.

> Quite a number of years ago I received a telephone call from L.A. A young man who told me, "I'm working on a ship as a seaman and I'm awfully afraid I'm going to go into orbit." I told him I thought it would be inadvisable to continue working on board that ship. So he got a job working in a *mine.* And he found that even if he were a mile deep into the earth he was still obsessed with the *fear* of going into orbit. And he came to Phoenix to see me. I don't know how he got my name or why he chose me, but I do know he saw a NUMBER of psychiatrists and they all wanted to give him *shock therapy*—electroshock therapy—because of his delusion that he was going to go into orbit. Now I didn't think he should get shock therapy. I had him get a job in a warehouse. And he was afraid he was going into orbit. And that delusion was so

persistent that he couldn't count as far as ten without
having to stop and reassure himself that he was not YET
in orbit. He was entitled to perspire because of the heat
but not perspire THAT much! But he was dreading so
much going into orbit. I tried to distract his mind by asking
him to count his steps as he walked along the street and
to memorize the street names. But that, "I'm going to go
into orbit, I'm going to go into orbit", obsessed him
. . . interfered with him. He couldn't get very much sleep
because he was afraid he was going to go into orbit. And
finally I realized I couldn't do anything for him except
settle down with him and EXPLAIN to him, "Now apparently it is your *destiny to go into orbit.* Now the as-
tronauts go into orbit, and there is always an end to the
orbit . . . they come back to earth again. And as long as
you are going to go into orbit why not get it OVER with?"
So I had him take salt pills and a canteen of water and I
had him walk about fourteen hours a day along the tops
of MOUNTAINS around here, and he had to come in at
10:30 at night to report that he had not yet gone into
orbit. But he slept *well,* as you would walking around on
mountain tops with a canteen of water and walking for
about fourteen hours a day. And finally he began to get
just a little bit dubious about going into orbit. Then his
sister came to me asking if he could go to California
where she lived. She said her husband had a job but that
he would not or could not fix up things around the house.
And she had a picket fence that needed some painting,
a gate that needed to be repaired, some shelves to be
built, and so I told the young man he could go to California because he would be in sight of mountains and he
could take his canteen with him and his salt pills, and if
he got a sudden feeling that he was destined to go into
orbit he could get up on top of a mountain so he could
go easily into orbit. Now a few months later he came

back and said, "That was a delusional psychotic idea" and he didn't know what had made him so crazy and he felt that I had saved him from hospitalization at the State hospital. And he decided that since I hadn't charged him for my services, he would give me a portable water bed. And gave us the name of the place where he got it. The man went out of business after being robbed five times. And the water bed was not well made . . . it sprang a leak so we salvaged the foam rubber and put it on my bed. And he got a job in Phoenix, and when winter came he comes over to me about going to Wisconsin and working as a lumber jack. I approved of it. For a couple of years he's been working very well, he came to see me recently and said, "I've realized how much you have done, I know you didn't charge me anything. That first water bed wasn't much good, so I've brought you these two cushions, this one and the one you enjoyed so much yesterday." He is married, his wife is a divorcee with one child, and he is certainly delighted in being a husband and a father. And you can't imagine the change in him from a hopelessly *desperate, fearful* young man to a confident, handsome young man who looks alert, IS alert and is enjoying life. So hope some young man who plans to go into orbit comes YOUR way.

This client's previous experiences with doctors, therapists, and acquaintances probably culminated in their either explicitly or implicitly discounting his belief that he might go into orbit. Of course, they reason, if you can convince him that his idea about being space-bound is erroneous then you will have solved the problem. In our experience, however, convincing someone by logic or exhortation that a long-held belief is mistaken is at least arduous, and often impossible. This is especially true when the belief being challenged is one which occupies a central role in the daily thoughts and actions of the individual. Regardless of the reality of the situation, the man in the above case believed he really was in danger of going into orbit. It was real for him and so, understandably, he would assume that any communication coming from those who tried to help him by discounting his belief came from individuals who did not trust his experiences to be valid. Our pre-orbiter then finds himself in the unfortunate bind of either distrusting his own senses or of distrusting theirs. Erickson was probably the first person that man confided in who responded as though the fear of going into orbit was to be taken seriously. Once established as an understanding and trustworthy person, Erickson could then move on to the question of what they were going to *do* about this dangerous situation, rather than get bogged down in arguing about whether or not the situation existed.

Behavioral Rapport

If need be, Erickson will go much further than simple verbal recognition of a client's beliefs. Whether as a function of those beliefs, a function of one's neurology, or a function of acquired habits, people engage in characteristic behaviors. How you sit, stand, and walk, how you strike up a conversation (or not), how and when you smile, frown, and become interested, are all examples of the myriad of behaviors in which you engage, and you do so in your own way—in a way that is characteristic of your own nervous system, training, and model of the world. It is the matching of these nuances of behavior that we previously mentioned under the topic of mirroring as an effective way of establishing rapport. In noticing and adjusting to these subtle tonal and kinaesthetic analogues (micro-behaviors) of your clients, however, the macro-behaviors might be overlooked. By "macro-behaviors" we are referring to those behaviors with which the individual's consciousness is involved at the time. For example, conversing with someone, angrily stomping around a room, and making puns at every opportunity are all examples of macro-behaviors, whereas your tonal pitch and tempo when conversing, the clenched teeth and fists when stomping about, and your oscillating eyebrows when punning are all micro-behaviors. The distinction is only important in drawing your attention to the possibility of responding to behavior as collections of many little chunks or as a few much larger, more encompassing chunks. The difference between the two in terms of utilization is that access of rapport through matching of micro-behaviors (mirroring) will, if done properly, be outside the conscious awareness of your client (most individuals are generally unaware of their ongoing analogue behavior), whereas your matching of macro-behaviors will almost always be consciously evident to the individual. If appropriately subtle in my behavior it is likely that it will go unnoticed by you that I clench my teeth each time you clench your own. However it is very *un*likely that you would fail to notice that each time you stomped around the room, I also stomped around the room. The obviousness of such macro-behavior mirroring to your client's conscious mind does not necessarily nullify its rapport value, but it does require that your micro-behavior (when matching your client's macro-behavior) be congruent with the intent or purpose of that behavior—that is, that your client's experience is that your reproduction of that behavior is for the client, rather than at his or her expense. For instance, in Erickson's encounter with the shy baby described earlier in this chapter, he did not even have the possibility of words and so had access only to behavior. Rather than exuding comraderie or "begging" for a response, Erickson first achieved rapport with the little girl by engaging in the same kind of shy behavior that she did. Once he had satisfactorily matched her own behavior, he was then free to evolve her towards more responsiveness. The following example of Erickson's use of behavioral rapport is exemplary in that his impact is strictly a function of his behavior.

You MEET people at their own level, just as you don't discuss philosophy with a baby learning to talk . . . you make NOISES at the baby. Now there was an autistic child at Arizona State Hospital. $50,000 had been raised and the child had been sent to Chicago for very special *care.* And a lot of psychiatrists, psychoanalysts worked with the child until the $50,000 was gone and they sent her back completely unchanged. One of my patients was rather lonesome and she liked to be a do-gooder and she visited the Arizona State Hospital, saw that ten year old girl, and finally persuaded the authorities to let the girl go for a walk with her. And that girl went with her, grimacing, and mouthing sounds, and grunting, and twisting and acting very peculiar. And this patient decided to bring her to see me. She brought her in. She had told me first about the girl and I told her, Yes, I'd see the girl. I assured her

I couldn't take the girl as a patient but I'd see the girl once. And she brought the girl in, and introduced the girl to me and me to the girl. And the girl made a number of weird sounds and so I REPLIED with weird sounds, and we grunted and groaned and squeaked and squawked for about half an hour. And then the girl answered a few simple questions and very promptly returned to her autistic behavior. And we really had a good time squeaking and squawking and grunting and groaning at each other. And then she took the patient back to the hospital. In the night time she took the patient for a walk. She told me later, "that girl almost pulled my *arm* off, yanking me down the street, she wanted to see *you* . . . the one man who could really talk her language."

In this example the macro-behavior is, of course, the girl's squeaking and squawking. Rather than conversing normally with her and attempting to get her to do likewise, Erickson adjusts *his* behavior, matching her squeak for squawk. For perhaps the first time, she had the opportunity to communicate with someone who spoke HER language, someone who made sense *to her.* It is important to also note that Erickson had a "really good time" squeaking and squawking with this girl as it is indicative of the *congruency* of Erickson's behavior. Any indication in Erickson's behavior that his mirroring of her squawking was exploitive, insincere, or derisive would certainly have been destructive of rapport. It was Erickson's willingness and ability to *congruently alter his OWN behavior* that made it possible for him to have the impact that he had on this girl.

Too often psychotherapists try to deal with their patients by using their doctoral degree language, trying to explain the ego, superego, and the id, conscious and unconscious, and the patient doesn't know whether you're talking about corn, potatoes or hash. Therefore, you try to use the language of the patient. Now a patient had been at Worcester for nine years. The patient had been brought in by the police with no identification marks on his clothing, we could get no information from him at all, we didn't know where he was from. There was no evidence he lived in Worcester. He might have been a transient. And for the nine years he was on the ward we'd be social and say "good morning". He replied with word salad, "bucket of lard, didn't pay up, sand on the beach" things like that . . . just irrelevant words all mixed up . . . didn't make any sense at all. And when I came there I was intrigued with that patient, intrigued by him. I endeavored many times to elicit his name, and all I ever got was a continuous outpouring of word salad. So I sent my secretary out and told her, "Take down his word salad and transcribe it for me." I went through that word salad and then I prepared a word salad similar to his but *not precisely* the same. And one morning at eight o'clock I said, "good morning" and he replied with a big paragraph of word salad to which I responded with a big paragraph of word salad. He responded and we "word-saladed" each other for a couple of hours. Finally he said, "Why don't you talk sense Dr. Erickson?" I said, "I'd be glad to, what is your name?" He told me. "Where are you from?" and I started taking a good history and all of a sudden he began his word salad again. So I responded in word salad. By the end of the day I had a complete history and medical examination—a very good account of him. And thereafter if I wanted to talk to him and he replied with word salad so did I. Well, he soon dropped his word salad. And within a year he was able to be released from the hospital and get a job. Now I certainly didn't do any therapy. I just met him at his own level. Now so many therapists . . . patients come to me and say, "My doctor said such and such. Now what did he mean?" And I'll have to explain it. In fact this is the way I began my private practice in Phoenix, answering questions the therapist or the doctor should have answered in the first place. And I probably got a lot of patient referrals.

Cultural Rapport

Part of everyone's world model is a cultural milieu, including those social and personal beliefs that are a function of your national, racial, religious, and sub-cultural history and present environment. In general, people who share similar backgrounds are more comfortable with, and trusting of, one another than those who do not. A sixteen-year-old delinquent will probably feel more relaxed around his buddies than he will around adults, a university professor is likely to feel out of place when among illiterate hill folk, and a navy man is not altogether at ease on an army base. Rapport is easier to establish between con-culturals because they share similar beliefs, vocabularies, macro-behaviors, and even analogue. For example, perhaps you can remember as a teenager using one vocabulary around your parents and a rather expanded and more colorful vocabulary when out with your friends. For many of us, being around our peers constituted a sub-culture that was substantially different from that of the family. Erickson is sensitive to the importance of his client's cultural background(s) and gracefully utilizes his knowledge of cultures and sub-cultures to help create the rapport necessary for impactful communication.

A woman in one of our seminars recounted the following excellent example of establishing rapport and a therapeutic relationship by matching a person's content and cultural world models: She was staying with friends when one evening the friend's little boy came running out of his room because there were "monsters in my room". His parents told him that there was no such thing as monsters and compelled him to return—crying—to his room. The next day the boy overcame a great deal of embarrassment and fear to ask the visitor if she thought there were such things as monsters. She became serious and replied that CERTAINLY there were monsters, *but that they were afraid of bed covers and of milk.* He was visibly relieved to hear this and reported the following morning that there had been monsters in his room that previous night but that he had pulled the covers over his head, and when he poked his head out a minute later the monsters had vanished! This is an excellent example of mirroring an individual's cultural model to create rapport, and then utilizing that cultural model to make the appropriate changes. The parent's pontifications about "reality" did nothing to change the *boy's* reality, serving only to begin him questioning either his parent's judgement or his own. Whether "true" or not, his parent's discounting of the existence of monsters was disrespectful of the boy's culture, for among children it is a well known fact that monsters are possible, if not prevalent.

Last summer I got a very worried letter from a young doctor who said, "A seven year old girl had developed sticky fingers. She had stolen some of her mother's jewelry and hid it in her bedroom, and had gone to camp and come back with eye glasses belonging to another girl. And we noticed that she *takes* things and *hides* them in her bedroom and we DON'T know how to handle it. Have you got any advice?" I wrote them back with instructions, and instructions for the father. I would write a letter to the little girl and put it in an envelope addressed to her and put THAT in an envelope addressed to *him* and sent it to his office. When he opened the envelope and saw a letter addressed to the daughter he should wait 'til midnight that night and drop it on her bedroom floor. And it was a letter from the seven-year-old growing up fairy, explaining that every child has a growing up fairy for *every year.* "Now the FIRST growing up fairy said some very nice things about you, the second year growing up fairy ALSO said some very nice things about you, so did the third, fourth, fifth, sixth year fairy. But maybe I'd better tell you what the growing up fairy looks like: I've got three left front feet and I write with the little left front foot. I've only got one right foot. And I've got eyes on the top of my head, in the back of my head, on each side and in the front of my head. That way I can see *everything!* I have two ears on each side of my head and a whole row of ears all along my back, all along my tail and on the tip of my tail is an ear . . . that's so I can *hear* everything that MY seven-year-old child does or says. I've got seven hind legs. I like to go barefoot but because it gets so hot in Phoenix I have to wear shoes on two of my hind feet in order to walk around. I use a shoe on my right front foot and on one of my left three feet. I like to go barefoot otherwise. I hear everything, I see everything. And I think you've been making mistakes. Of course you're apt to make some mistakes. After you make them, you CORRECT them." And she had her mother read it. Of course the mother was prepared. The mother and father were very mystified by the little girl's concern. They agreed there was a growing up fairy for every child. And then she had ANOTHER letter. It said, "You tell your mother that she has to make you peanut butter pancakes using buttermilk in the pancakes and peanut butter. *All* seven year old's growing up fairies have to eat at least ONE breakfast of buttermilk, peanut butter pancakes." Her mother made them, obedient to that letter. Then I got a letter. I told her she could communicate to me by writing me a letter, giving it to her father who knew a mailman who could deliver the letter to me. I got invited to her eight-year-old birthday. I wrote back, "I'd LIKE to, but her eight-year-old growing up fairy was taking over. I was *glad* she had corrected ALL her mistakes. It's a lot of fun doing that." And with very youthful patients it is very effective. Even now I have children call me up or the parents call me up and say, "Will you please call my children and play Santa Claus to them the way you did when *I* was a child?"

As in the monster example, Erickson responds to this seven-year-old within her *own* sub-culture, "youngsterdom." For a child "laws" are outside of their experience and, so, irrelevant. But *fairies,* now there is something that makes sense, that is something to pay attention to. The points to be made here are essentially the same as those made in the two previous sections. That is, a prerequisite for effective interactions with your clients is rapport, that rapport is your client knowing that you comprehend (not "like") their model of the world, and that rapport can be created by mirroring your clients' models of the world at any one (some, or all) of many possible levels, including that of "culture." In this next example, Erickson utilizes his knowledge of a convict's sub-culture to establish rapport. Note that mirroring this convict's sub-culture does not necessarily entail continually acting like a convict, only that one be able to verbally or behaviorally acknowledge and/or utilize features of that sub-culture when appropriate and useful.

> Do you know what the Seventh Step House is? It's a half-way house for ex-convicts. And I worked my way through medical school by examining penal and correctional inmates in Wisconsin. So I've always been interested in the subject of crime, and of course I'm a member of Seventh Step and they referred Paul to me. Paul was all of six feet tall, a very handsome man and a well-built man. He came in and said, "I'm an ex-con and Seventh Step sent me to you to straighten me out." Paul was thirty-two years old and he spent twenty years of his life locked up. So I spent an hour discussing the situation with him and at the end of the hour Paul said, politely, "Do you know where you can shove that?" and left. His girlfriend brought him back. He listened politely for another hour, and then said politely, "You know where you can shove THAT!" Now for seven months he lived off his girlfriend. She lodged and boarded him. He worked as a bouncer in various taverns to pay for his drinks. At the end of seven months his girlfriend got tired of his failure to contribute anything, of his being drunk every night, and the tavern keepers were fed up with his brawling. So they threw him OUT. And Paul walked from his girlfriend's home to here . . . temperature of 109 degrees and a six mile walk and he had certainly been drunk the night before. He came in and said, "What was that you had to say to me?" I repeated what I had to say . . . he listened politely for an hour then said, "You know where you can shove *that,*" and left. Walked back to his girlfriend's home, begged for a second chance, she said, "NO",

went to the tavern keepers begged them for a second chance, they all said, "No", so he walked back. A total of eighteen miles walking with a *terrible* hangover . . . came in and said, "What was that you had to say to me?" I said, "Paul, I've shoved it. Now the only thing I can do for you is tell you I've got a big back yard. There is an old mattress out there, you can sleep on that. If you're cold, and I don't think it will be cold, my wife will furnish you a blanket. If it rains, and I don't think it is going to rain, you can pull your mattress under the eaves. But you stay in that back yard and think things over." As we went through the gate into the back yard I said, "And Paul, if you want me to confiscate your boots you'll have to *beg* me to." He didn't beg me to so I didn't take his boots away. Paul didn't realize it but I know enough about convict honor and that I put him on his convict's honor not to run away. Paul spent the night there. I told him there was an outdoor faucet and in the morning rap on the kitchen door and Mrs. Erickson will give you a can of pork and beans. The next day my daughter Kristina and my fifteen year old granddaughter Micky came home from Michigan and they saw this great big hulk of a man. He had a *horrible scar* covering his chest. And they both wanted to know "who was that man in your backyard?" I said, "It's Paul. He is an ex-convict and he is sobering up in the backyard. He is staying there as long as he wishes." And my daughter said (Paul was nude to the waist), and my daughter said, "That SCAR on his chest, how did he get it?" I said, "I don't know, I didn't inquire." "Would it be all right if I talk to him?" I said, "Yes" and my granddaughter's eyes bugged out at the thought of seeing a real live ex-convict. So the two girls went out to talk to Paul, and Paul was lonesome. And he poured out his soul to them. And Kristina said, "What would you like for dinner tonight?" And Paul said, "I'd like a half of a pint but I know I'm not going to get it." She said, "You're so right. What would you like other than a half of a pint?" Paul said, "Anything." Well Kristina is a gourmet cook, and she went ALL out preparing a gourmet meal such as he'd never tasted before. And he slept better that night. My son has a Basset, short legged, and that Basset would climb up the side of the Paloverde tree to get an elevated view of life. And Paul looked at that low slung, stump-legged dog laboriously climbing up to get a better view of the world and he became his favorite. Paul stayed there four nights and four days and asked my permission could he go to his girlfriend's home. He had an old junk car parked in his girlfriend's driveway. He thought he could fix it up and sell it for $25.00. That'd give him a stake, so I told him to go ahead. He fixed it up and sold it, returned to sleep the night in the backyard. And he asked my permission the next day if he could go out and hunt for a job. He came back and had located two jobs. One was a horse wrangler, didn't pay well, which he wanted and a factory job which paid well but he wasn't terribly interested in. So he spent the night thinking it over. In the meantime Kristina had been talking to him, she found out how he got that *scar.* He was committing an armed robbery and a policeman shot him in the heart. He was taken to the emergency room. They did emergency open heart surgery. And that's why he had that horrible scar. Paul later told me, "I don't understand those two girls. They don't BELONG in this world. I've never seen that kind of girl before. They are entirely different. I can't understand them. *They don't belong in my world.''* After thinking it over he had decided on the factory job, asked my permission to go. He took the job. He had $25.00. He rented a room, and on Thursday he called his girlfriend and said, "Come along with me, we are going to Alcoholics Anonymous." And Paul has now been sober for four years and his girlfriend sobered up too. And the only therapeutic thing I said was, "You want me to confiscate your boots you'll have to *beg* me to."

You have to hit patients in the right *way* in order to get them to accept therapy. They want SOME change . . . they don't know what KIND of change. They don't know how to MAKE the change. All you do is create a situation that's favorable and say "giddy-up" and keep their nose on the road. The last time I saw Paul he was enjoying life *thoroughly* . . . a good solid citizen.

Footnotes

1. For a complete description of the identification, significance and utilization of predicates see: Grinder and Bandler, *The Structure of Magic, Vol. II;* Bandler, Grinder, and Delozier, *Patterns of the Hypnotic Techniques of Milton H. Erickson, M.D., Vols. I and II;* Gordon, *Therapeutic Metaphors;* Cameron-Bandler, *They Lived Happily Ever After;* and Dilts, et al, *Neuro-Linguistic Programming, Vol. I.*

2. Again, you can find examples and a model of Erickson's utilization of these patterns in Grinder, Delozier, and Bandler's *Patterns of the Hypnotic Techniques of Milton H. Erickson, M.D., Vol. II.*

CHAPTER 4

The Touchstone

Reference Frame Interventions

I tell those who complain about insomnia, "Insomnia is your misuse of time . . . those are bonus hours. While you are awake in bed start thinking about all of the pleasant things that you want to do, that you have done, and you'll find that they are bonus hours, not insomnia hours. So you'll find yourself with thoughts of something pleasant, your body will become accustom to the bed, and you'll go to sleep."

There is a black stone used to test the purity of gold and silver. When a sample of the metal to be tested is scratched across the surface of this stone the characteristic streak of color left behind reveals the quality of that sample. This dark stone is called the touchstone. For the testing of the metal of our experiences as human beings we use the touchstone of our personal sets of criteria.

The one endeavor human beings are always engaged in is that of making sense out of their ongoing experiences with respect to their personal models of the world. "Making sense" out of an experience is an interpretive process which culminates in an individual either accessing an appropriately comprehensive generalization regarding the significance of an experience or compels the creation of a new under-standing capable of satisfactorily describing the experience. If, for example, a friend comes up to you and pinches you on the arm, how you respond to that experience, both in terms of your internal state and your external behavior, will depend upon how you interpret your friend's act. If on the basis of the context you and your friend are in, his behavior just prior to the pinch, his facial expressions during the pinch, and your personal history with being touched in that way, you interpret his gesture as being a "reprimand" you will undoubtedly respond to him and the situation differently than if you divined that pinch to be an invitation to play, a token of friendship, or a gesture of affection. So a client seats himself in Milton Erickson's office and complains bitterly that he is suffering from an unfortunate condition —insomnia. For him the experience of not being able to quickly drop off to sleep "means" that he has a PROBLEM with sleeping, which meaning will, of course, lead him to respond to "going to sleep" with certain kinds of internal states (eg. dread, frustration) and external behaviors (eg. counting sheep, taking pills). After listening to his client's plight Erickson then completely changes the situation from an unfortunate PROBLEM to a fortuitous opportunity with the deft stroke, "Insomnia is your misuse of time . . . those are bonus hours." To the authors, after listening to many hours of Erickson's descrip-tions of therapeutic work, few statements typify his orientation and skill as much as the deceptively simple, "Insomnia is your misuse of time . . . those are bonus hours." With those few words Erickson completely reorients his client with respect to the "problem situation" so that what has for so long seemed a millstone is suddenly revealed as a valuable piece of antique jewelry. This is much more than simple idea play. It is this shift in perspective, as revealed by Erickson to his sleepless client, that will make it possible for Erickson to lead that person to more useful bedtime experiences. This skill in the alchemy of viewpoints constitutes the second hub about which Erickson's ther-apeutic interventions turn.

Criteria

The question is asked both explicitly and implicitly in many ways and by all of us, "What gets people to behave in the ways that they do?" One way of answering this question is to think of behavior as the manifest function of the interpretations an individual applies to his or her ongoing experience. In the example above, for instance, how a person will respond both internally and externally to being pinched on the arm will depend upon the significance with which that experience is imbued. Similarly, your internal and external responses with respect to an offer of a cocktail, having a headache, being faced with an exam, asking a loved one for a favor, and every other example of experiential input can be attributed to the particular perspectives you adopt regarding those inputs. How, then, is it possible that two people can take the same test, and one be terrified of it and the other look forward to the experience?

There is a curious idea rampant and rarely challenged in the world that there are such things as "bad" and "good" experiences. What do you consider to be a "bad" experience? Perhaps taking a test? If so, how is it possible that for some people the taking of a test is an exciting opportunity to extend oneself or find out what one knows? What is, for you, an example of a "good" experience? Dancing perhaps? But for some individuals the very thought of dancing fills them with horror at such exhibitionism. The list could, of course, go on forever. Virtually any experience or behavior you might identify will elicit any number of divergent responses from different people. Obviously these experiences and behaviors are not inherently good, bad, better, best, or right—they are indifferent. They are just experiences. What distinguishes each of them as something to be cherished and sought (or feared and avoided) is the individual perspective with which each is viewed.

In order to adjust your behavior appropriately you are continually evaluating both consciously and unconsciously your ongoing input (experiences) with respect to some set of standards or perspectives. The impact of the unconscious application of one's perspective on input is certainly evident if a speeding car were to be bearing down on you right now. The perspective that "one's life must be protected" will make it possible for (in fact, compel) you to jump out of the way. (The authors were referred a client who had been seized by authorities while nonchalantly strolling in front of freeway traffic. HIS perspective, he told us, was, "It's irrelevant whether I live or die," and so he did not bother to get out of the way of speeding cars.) Your conscious invocation of your particular perspective is probably more evident. If a person approaches you asking that you help him steal food from a supermarket, your response to him will depend upon your perspective on the appropriateness of the requested behavior. Some people will say

"No, I won't help you," some will call the police, but some will say, "Sure!" If your perspective is that it is wrong to steal then upon evaluating the stranger's request your answer will probably be "No." If, instead, you believe that stealing is a legitimate way of acquiring things then your answer might be "Yes." Same input ("help me steal"), different perspectives (it's right—it's wrong), nets you different responses ("let's do it"—"I'm calling the police"). The content of these differing perspectives, then, constitute the criteria (standards) by which the significance of an experience is determined.

Any time you must make a judgement about something (which, technically speaking, is ALL the time, as you are always evaluating input) you will have to apply your personal criteria to the experience in order to sort out just how you should respond. In the example above, how you would respond (that is, either agree to steal or call the police) is a function of your criteria with respect to "stealing". Seems pretty clear, right? Suppose, however, this would-be thief goes on to say that he hates to do it, but his two-month old baby is starving to death? Of course, you now must also evaluate his request with respect to whatever criteria you have about the preservation of life, children, and unwilling thieves. Now, you still might not help him steal, but your internal response and behavior towards him will certainly be different. As each piece of experiential input presents itself to you (originating either in the external world or from internal processes), the criteria which are relevant to that input are accessed and utilized to evaluate that experience and, thereby, determine your response.

The effect of criteria on the implementation of behavior becomes evident when one travels to a foreign country. For instance, among some groups of peoples in India it is considered reprehensible to make direct requests of another individual. It is instead highly valued to be able to talk "around" a request until the recipient perceives its drift. Among these Indians, an American who had learned to be "straight" with his or her communications would, of course, commit a horrendous *faux pas* by directly asking for directions to the nearest town— *not* because directly asking for directions is *inherently* anti-social behavior, but because those individuals being asked utilize criteria that judge directness as being discourteous. All experience is simply data until you apply appropriate criteria to it, at which point its significance is defined. For a particular individual, "Help me steal" or "What's the quickest way to Naini Tal?" are neither good nor bad, right nor wrong, until that person evaluates those statements with respect to his or her criteria in relation to stealing and answering direct requests for directions.

The point is that events that are continually occurring in both the internal and external world are in and of themselves neutral, and that what gives those events significance is the conscious and/or unconscious application of relevant criteria to evaluate them. And the result of that evaluation will determine one's behavior in response to that event.

Identifying Criteria

How do you identify the criteria that a person is using in evaluating ongoing experience? Anytime you engage in judging information or experience you will necessarily access whatever criteria are relevant to that content area. For instance, answer the following question:

What do you like about your best friend?

Your answer may go something like, "he/she is fun loving, cares about my feelings, and is interested in many of the same things I am". This answer identifies some highly valued criteria for the individual who said it, that is, what this person highly values—fun, respect, and shared interests—in relation to friendship. In determining whether or not a particular acquaintance is indeed a "friend", this person will evaluate whether or not that acquaintance's behaviors fulfill the criteria of being capable of fun, respect, and the sharing of interests. Acquaintances who are fun loving but are disrespectful of personal feelings when in pursuit of that fun will probably not be considered as being "friends" by this evaluator. Again, criteria are those standards or rules that are highly valued by an individual and are therefore used by that person to make discriminations about the personal significance of experiences. For instance: "It is important to *exercise.*" "One should be *direct.*" "*Fun* is important." "Is that *useful?*" "Which would be the *most fun* to do?" "I want the *best.*" "*Waste* is *awful.*" "*Appearances* are important." "Which is *more comfortable?*" "*Congruency* makes the difference."

From the moment an individual walks into your office he or she will be demonstrating and describing to you a great many of their valued criteria (perspectives) about the world and how that world is organized. These beliefs range from such automatic and mundane premises as the safety of sitting down in a chair (because it resembles a class of things to be sat on) to the conscious and cosmic considerations of life after death, what constitutes truth, love, and beauty, and so on. The things that a person does and the things that a person says presuppose certain viewpoints held consciously or unconsciously regarding how the world is organized, that is, what things, behaviors, and ideas are right and wrong, important and unimportant, useful and not useful, good and bad. Taken together, these criteria constitute that person's *model of the world,* and will be evident in that person's verbal and behavioral responses. For example, we once overheard the following conversation by the losing team at the conclusion of a hard-fought ball game:

> #26: (throwing some equipment down) "Bastards must've cheated!"
> #16: "Damn! Lost by one point . . . one lousy point!"
> #13: (brightly) "Yeah. Great game, wasn't it?" (At which point #13 was jumped by the rest of the team and, uh, re-educated with respect to the proper responses to competition and losing.)

#13's teammates correctly understood from his remark that he considered playing *well* more important than winning. If the other team members had world models similar to #13's they might have left the playing field happy and satisfied, rather than angry and frustrated. We especially want to point out to you here that we are NOT saying that the rest of the team should be like #13, but that (1) all verbal and analogical behavior is indicative of an individual's model of the world and that (2) different world models produce different outcomes in terms of personal experiences. And as anyone who has listened to a political debate for even a moment knows, the certainty that one individual feels about his own view of the world is often confronted and matched by that of others whose beliefs about the world, although very different, are felt to be equally certain. It seems general and accepted knowledge that different people may hold different views in response to the same subject, and yet we know of several individuals who believe so strongly in this diversity of perspective that they are compelled to defend and argue its veracity with someone who does NOT believe in it! It is both ironic and important to understand that very often these same individuals deny *themselves* a similar latitude and flexibility in regards to their own personal beliefs. Mr. Smith can temporize that some people say that football provides a necessary outlet for aggression, and then turn around and see his insomnia as only a bad thing, a malady to be disposed of.

Sorting and Re-Sorting

Clearly, many things in the world are good or bad depending on HOW you look at them. Change in therapy always involves some change in perspective. In their sincere desire to preserve their client's integrity many therapists operate under the injunction that it is important to maintain and not compromise one's beliefs, and at the same time they press their clients towards "change". This places a severe burden on both the therapist and the client. Almost the only therapeutic alternative open to a therapist who believes that one should not have to change beliefs is to assist his clients to learn to accept themselves the way they are (even then, however, the therapist is changing the client's belief that *the present state is unacceptable*). Of course there may be virtue in self-acceptance, but as an overriding therapeutic model it has some important limitations. For example, a therapist working out of that model and faced with a married couple who are complaining about their seemingly incompatible needs has the choice of either assisting them in accepting their incongruent needs and living with that schism OR of splitting-up to find other partners that are already matched for their needs. The result of the first choice is usually the continued *tolerance* of an unsatisfactory situation, while the second results in the dissolution of a relationship and the probability of a futile search for that "perfect mate".

Everything that constitutes an individual human being is stored as that person's generalizations, beliefs, behaviors, needs and the rest. The pervasiveness of one's generalizations is often taken for granted because of the subtly of their expression. For instance, when you go to sit in a chair you don't test it out first to discover whether or not it will bear sitting. Part of your model of the world is that anything shaped like "that" is sitable. You certainly were not born with that knowledge, and now there is no need to consciously consider it. The catalogue which completely contained any one individual's model of the world would be impossibly massive, but erase that catalogue and you would have nothing more than some flesh and bones. Generalizations about the nature of the world are created and refined by external and internal behaviors, and *at the same time* one's generalizations influence the characteristics of one's internal and external behavior.

It is clear, then, that a change in one's behavior will result in some change in those generalizations with which it is connected, and that a change in an individual's generalizations within a particular context will result in corresponding changes in the behavior which it generates. In fact, one of the generalizations we have generated out of our experiences as therapists and modelers is that it is impossible to separate a change in one's behavior (i.e. responses, thoughts, feelings, actions, etc.) from changes in personal beliefs about "the way the world is". They are the proverbial chicken and egg. There are times when external or internal environmental circumstances compel new behavior which then results in alterations of one's model of the world (a detour forces you to find a new way to work, through which you "discover" the importance of *variety*), and there are times when resorting one's model of the world results in new behaviors (in thinking about your humdrum existence you "realize" that what you need is *variety*, and so you begin finding different ways to work each day). Chapter V is about the former (the chicken) and this chapter is about the latter (the egg).

A summary of the points we have been making so far is that your behavior and internal experience in response to any piece of input will depend upon the criteria you bring to bear in evaluating that input. We also gave examples of how two different individuals evaluating the same input will respond differently by virtue of their differing criteria in relation to it. However, we do not mean to imply by these examples of individually characteristic cause(criteria)-effect(responses) relationships that the response of an individual is, though unique, somehow inflexible. As was demonstrated in the stealing example above, it is also the case that an individual's responses within a certain context will vary depending upon what criteria (plural) are being accessed at that time. That is, all of us are capable of accessing different sets of criteria if additional input warrants it or if instructed to do so. For example, in our example above the response of the person being asked to steal changed as new information was revealed to him, each piece of which accessed in him new sets of (suddenly) relevant criteria. This accessing of relevant criteria we call SORTING. That is, as information comes in, the individual sorts through his experience searching for the criteria that are relevant to the evaluation that he must make. It is like folding laundry, in that if you want to fold the socks first you sort through the pile looking for any clothing that looks like a sock. When you can find no more socks then you may switch to sorting for underwear. These ways of sorting laundry make "sense" in terms of most peoples' experience, but they are NOT the only possibilities in terms of sorting laundry. You could be asked to sort your laundry with respect to color similarity, or in terms of ascending size, or in terms of age similarity, and so on. AND you could probably sort your laundry in any of these ways *without ever having done or thought of it before.* That is, you understand the discriminations of "same color," "ascending size," and "same age," but you had never before accessed those particular ways of sorting in relation to the context of folding laundry—it had never *occurred* to you to do it. But once asked it is easily done. And when you DO re-sort your laundry with respect to one of the criteria suggested above you end up with piles of laundry that are different than those you are accustomed to having. Similarly, Erickson makes it possible for the insomniac to respond differently to his sleeplessness by teaching that person to sort for how his wakefulness is an *opportunity,* rather than how it is a problem. Although each of us characteristically sorts for certain criteria in relation to certain contexts, we are all capable of sorting for and utilizing *novel* criteria in relation to those same contexts when those criteria are appropriately accessed. This is also known as changing one's "perspective" or "frame of reference", and we now turn to how Erickson assists others to re-sort their experience in useful ways.

Sorting for Assets

The point has been made that the criteria an individual uses to evaluate his ongoing internally and externally generated experience will exert a profound influence on that person's corresponding internal state and behavior. People who view themselves as clumsy oafs will walk, move and respond to others differently than those individuals who believe themselves to be graceful. The perspective from which you view yourself and the world also makes it possible for your environment to verify and reinforce that perspective. A "clumsy oaf" declines invitations to dance or participate in sports, while "Mr. Graceful" may think learning to wield a chainsaw an unthinkable task. It is precisely because of this tremendous effect of perspective on behavior that Erickson frequently takes care to change his client's presently limiting perspective to a frame of reference capable of providing a wider range of more satisfying experiences.

Good businessmen know how to take liabilities generated during the natural progress of their business and turn them into assets of some kind. Erickson is a master at turning behavioral and characterological liabilities into assets. He operates out of the model we have been describing, that is, that what makes a personal characteristic or behavior a problem is not necessarily inherent in that characteristic or behavior but is a function of the perspective (set of criteria) employed in evaluating it. This model not only frees Erickson from being trapped into judging the characteristrics and behaviors of others as being good or bad, it also leads to the proposition that a person's behavior can be changed by altering his or her perspective. If you are able to substantially affect an individual's perspective with respect to a particular content area you will effect a corresponding change in that person's behavior. Here, now, is an example of how Erickson turns a liability into an asset:

Now when I arrived in Michigan at Wayne County Hospital I encountered a most unusual person. A young girl, medical technician, rather pretty, well-formed except she had the biggest, HUGEST fanny I had ever seen on any girl. And when she walked down the corridor I noticed that when she passed somebody she'd swing her fanny angrily toward that person. Well that interested me. So I made it a point to keep an eye open 'cause I wanted to see what that girl is going to DO with that great big fanny of hers. And I noticed that every visiting day was her *day off* and at the entrance of the grounds she met the mothers and their children . . . always asked the mother if she could give the children a piece of gum, a piece of candy, a toy, and volunteered to take care of the children while the mother visited the patient. And for a whole year that went on. That seemed to be her entire life, looking after those visitor children, and she gave every evidence of making that her one and only joy in life. So that gave me ANOTHER idea about her. Then one day she suddenly developed the hiccups. She hiccupped night and day. We had a staff of 169 physicians, they all examined her and could find nothing wrong with her and they finally told her she would have to have a psychiatrist consultation. She knew what THAT meant. I'd be the psychiatrist called in and she politely refused to have a psychiatrist called in. So, she was informed she was being hospitalized in Wayne County Hospital for free and receiving her pay, "you're paid even though you're not working, everything is being taken care of for you as if you were fully employed. If you're not going to take medical advice just resign your position, call a private ambulance and go to a private hospital and get over the hiccups there!" She thought that over and said she'd permit me to see her. So at two o'clock that afternoon I walked into her room, closed the door behind me, and said, "Keep your mouth shut! Listen! I've got a few things to say to you and I want you to listen 'cause you need an understanding. I KNOW you've got the biggest fanny in creation. I KNOW you don't like it but it IS yours. And you like children, therefore you'd like to get married, have children of your own. And you're afraid that great big fanny of yours is a *barrier* . . . that's your *error.* You haven't read the Song of Solomon. You SHOULD have read your bible. The pelvis is mentioned as the *cradle of children.* " I said, "The man who will want to marry you will not see a great big fat fanny . . . he'll see a wonderful cradle for children." She listened quietly. "Men who want to father children DO want a nice cradle for the child." And when I finished my speech I said, "You can think it over. After I leave keep on hiccupping. There is no reason for anybody except you and I to *know* you don't NEED those hiccups. You have something of great VALUE so let your hiccups disappear around 10:30 tonight, 11 o'clock, that way nobody will say a psychiatrist cured you, that my interview was an utter failure." So her hiccups disappeared around that time. She went back to work and one day at lunch time while my secretary was having lunch she came into

my office and said, "Here is something I want you to
see." She showed me her engagement ring. She said, "I
thought you should be the first person to see this." Sometime later she privately brought a young man into the
office to meet me—her fiance. They were married shortly
and started raising a family. Now reorientation of thinking
. . . I called her fanny a great big fat fanny, as big as I had
ever seen. I told her she hated it, but she didn't *understand* it. Then I presented it as a cradle for children
against my background of knowing how much she liked
children. And how a man who would want to father
children WOULD want a nice cradle for children. Now
I didn't need to go into the past, I could just discuss the
current state of *affairs* . . . reorienting her thinking, reorienting her thinking in accord with her own secret desires.
I was unafraid to call her fanny a big fat fanny, so she
knew I was telling the truth, so she could believe what I
said. I don't like doctors who pussyfoot around and try
to say things sweetly and gently. The truth should be told
simply, straight-forward fashion because that is the ONLY
way the patient is actually going to absorb therapy and
proceed to benefit. And once you get them reoriented,
their nose pointed down the road, they'll go.

As Erickson says, what he did here was to reorient the woman's
thinking with respect to her fanny. She felt that the size of her fanny
was a social hindrance, so of course it became a social hindrance in
reality. There is no reason for her to attempt to establish relationships
with men *since* she knows they won't like her fanny. When Erickson
realizes that she wants children he re-educates her regarding her fanny
—it is not an undesirably fat fanny but a *cradle* for children. Because
of her obviously highly valued "secret desire" for children, Erickson
knows that this new perspective will be one which can probably eclipse
the old perspective and will be one which she can embrace. Consider
the following description of how Erickson structured his reorientation
of this woman with the huge fanny: Erickson identified some aspect

of her present model of the world which she highly valued (having children), then described her unwanted characteristic (a fat fanny) as being a RESOURCE towards achieving that highly valued end. In our example case, for instance, regardless of whether or not Erickson's statement about men seeing a "wonderful cradle" is true, he knows that if *she* believes it to be true that new generalization will have a profound effect on her subsequent behavior around men. As a woman with a "desirable and wonderful cradle for children", she will certainly respond to men in ways which are different from a woman who considers herself unattractive. New responses in the woman's behavior will, of course, elicit new responses from others, which experiences in turn will reinforce those behaviors and will probably stimulate other novel and appropriate responses. And so the snowball becomes an avalanche.

What, then, made it possible for Erickson to get the snowball rolling in the first place? Of course, Erickson did more than simply tell the woman in the above example, "Actually, you really are attractive . . . No, really!" Everyone has had the (frustrating) experience of attempting to persuade another person that what they considered awful about themselves was not awful at all. But these sincere efforts rarely transpire with results as gratifying as those enjoyed by Erickson. Usually such interchanges degenerate into a fruitless form of reassurance ("No really, you ARE attractive . . ."), with the result that the friend or client is even more convinced that they are indeed deficient. Consider your own experience regarding some deficiency you believe or at one time believed you had. You thought you were too short or too tall, unattractive, not doing well at something, and so on. If you now recall any attempts by interested friends or associates at persuading you that you really weren't "that way", . . . how successful were they? Probably not very, you thanked them for their words and concern, and went on believing whatever you started with (with the possible exception that you were even more sure of your deficiency— why else would they have been so intent upon persuading you otherwise?) The point is that changing a person's perspective is obviously more involved than simply enjoining them to think differently.

The first thing of importance for us to recognize in what Erickson did with this woman is in regards to how he established rapport with her. He did NOT tell her she did not have a huge fanny or that it was attractive. Instead, Erickson paced her experience by agreeing with her that it was indeed "the biggest fanny in creation." We wish to reemphasize that rapport is not a function of whether or not someone likes you. It is a function of your client being able to trust your communications to (and about) them. Erickson understands that by telling his client that he is aware that she has a huge fanny he will reassure her that she can depend upon the veracity of his judgements (after all, he is agreeing with her own perceptions). So, Erickson first establishes rapport by pacing her own perceptions of herself. Erickson then identifies for her something that she highly values, something out of her own model of the world—the desire to have children—and then causally connects her not having children with her perspective on her fanny. That is, "My great big fat fanny prevents me from having children." All of these statements serve to further pace her experience and to enhance rapport between her and Erickson, who is demonstrating an obvious understanding of her situation by virtue of his observations. Erickson goes on to tell her that she is wrong about her fanny, which not only paces her own desires (that is, to be wrong about having an unattractive fanny), but also suddenly puts her on Erickson's side for, of course, she would like him to be right about her being wrong about her fanny. Erickson completes the sequence by describing her fanny in a way that is both reasonable and is coincident with her own desires. Now when she thinks about her fanny she can consider how it is a wonderful cradle, rather than an eyesore.

The significance of Erickson's rapport maneuvers is that they made it possible for him to secure from the woman the credibility he would require in order for her to accept the alteration in perspective that he proposes. There is more to Erickson's intervention than simply establishing rapport, however. As Erickson himself says, she is "afraid that great big fat fanny of yours is a barrier [to having children] . . ." Erickson here is identifying what is, in her model of the world, a cause-effect relationship between the size of her fanny and her attractiveness to men. That is, her perspective is that her large fanny causes her to be unattractive. Whether or not she "really" IS unattractive to men is beside the point. As long as she believes that she is she will not only act as though she is unattractive, but may not even notice when others ARE attracted to her.

When a client presents you with a cause-effect statement such as "my large fanny makes me unattractive" you can either accept the cause-effect relationship as stated by the client, or do something to change it. (Remember that a cause-effect relationship or "belief", as stated by another person, matching your own model of the world is

NOT a comment on the truth, importance, or value of that shared belief. Different people have different ideas about the way things are, and if you are going to help them alter those beliefs in a way that permits them to to realize more satisfying experiences in life then you must, as did Erickson, be able to think about frames of reference and their effects within and in relation to that individual, rather than in relation to your own—arbitrary—standards.) Accepting the client's cause-effect description means that your efforts will be directed towards changing the "cause" (that is, making her fanny smaller) and in so doing, meet that person's criteria (in our example, her criteria for attractiveness). If you do not accept the stated cause-effect relationship then you can do what Erickson did, which was to make the cause a cause leading to some other, more desireable effect (that is, her fanny becomes the cause of her being attractive to men who want children). Again, the difference between the two choices we have just described is that you can either change the physical/behavioral characteristic about which the client is complaining in such a way as to match his/her criteria for acceptability, or you can let that physical/-behavioral characteristic stand, changing instead the individual's perspective with regards to it. There is an obvious choice as to when you would want to alter an individual's perspective rather than tackle his or her body or behavior, that being when the "cause" of your client's unwanted present state is something that is either outside of his/her control or would be inappropriate to alter. In the case of the woman with the huge fanny, Erickson chose to change her perspective with respect to her fanny, rather than attempt the awesome task of making her fanny fit her criteria for beauty. Erickson does this by making the attribute that she finds so offensive (her fat fanny) a means to a highly valued end that he has already identified out of her own model of the world (having children). The idea that her fanny was a resource for achieving her goal of having children naturally led to changes in her behavior, which naturaly led to changes in the kinds of responses she elicited from others, which, of course, naturally led to marriage and pregnancy.

To recap, what is important about changing a person's perspective is that in so doing that person is given the opportunity to discover new behavioral and conceptual resources which are more useful, appropriate, and satisfying. One way in which Erickson does this is to describe a client's unwanted behavior or characteristic as being a resource which makes possible the realization or expression of some other realm of possible experience already highly valued by that person. The context in which this particular format is useful is in those cases in which the physical or behavioral attribute with which the client is concerned is either beyond his or her control in terms of changing or would not be useful to change. It is not particularly significant whether or not the connection created between the unwanted present state and the highly valued reference frame "family" is in reality spurious (your ability to secure and maintain rapport is crucial in this regard). What is important is that transforming that unwanted present state into a resource makes it possible for the person to respond differently to the world and, so, discover new possibilities in experience (that is, by virtue of the effects of the new behaviors that are inherent in the new perspective). We wish to emphasize that what made it possible for Erickson to have the impact that he had on this fat-fannied woman was the interaction of rapport AND framing patterns. Neither being in rapport nor offering a new perspective is in and of itself sufficient to create a new idea in another person. The new perspective is the wheel, rapport the grease.

Following is an algorithm which will enable you to reproduce this pattern in your own work:

The first step is to identify the stated (supposed) cause-effect relationship between some behavior/characteristic and the client's inability to achieve some desired state. That is, what does the individual believe to be the "cause" of his difficulties? If that behavior/characteristic is either beyond the client's control, or it would not be useful for the individual to change it, or it is not worth the effort it would take to change it, then proceed with this pattern—if that behavior/characteristic is something that can itself be changed and you agree that it would be useful to do so, refer to the pattern in the next section. (For example, the fat-fannied lady believes her bottom to be a barrier to having a family. Assuming an absence of genetic or pathological precursors, the size of her fanny is something that is possible for her to control, and it would probably be useful for her to have slimmer hips. But Erickson does not have the time that it would take to alter her weight, thereby making her body fit her criteria for attractiveness, and so he makes her criteria fit her huge fanny in a way that makes possible the kind of behavior she wants and needs to have in order to achieve her desired familied state.) So:

1. Identify the cause-effect relationship as believed by the individual.
(in our example) Her huge fanny "makes" her unattractive to men.

The next piece of information you need to identify for yourself is what highly valued desired state does your client believe is precluded by the cause-effect relationship he or she has identified, or to what highly valued desired state within that person's model of the world could the unwanted behavior/characteristic possibly be connected by you. So:

2. Identify some highly valued desired state or criterion to which the unwanted behavior/characteristic is (or could be) connected.
She wants a family.

3. Pace your client's experience by explicitly stating your understanding of what he or she identifies as being the cause and effect of his or her problem situation.
Erickson tells the woman that he knows she has "the biggest fanny in creation."

Erickson is now on the verge of presenting his client with a new perspective with respect to the problem situation which, if accepted by that person, will make it possible for her to respond in the world with more useful and rewarding internal experiences and external behaviors. But of course the success of this intervention rests on Erickson's ability to get his client to accept *Erickson's* version of "reality". The importance of rapport in this regard has already been described. Erickson goes further, however, and elicits in his client an internal state of defending one's behavior or beliefs. What this maneuver does is insure that when his client does re-sort her perspective with respect to the new frame of reference that that re-sorting is accompanied by a profoundly affecting and undeniable shift in internal experience, a shift that is unlikely to occur in someone starting instead from an "uncommitted" internal state. That is, if you are not thoroughly committed to a particular position (ie. wishy-washy) when someone proposes to you a different and compellingly (because of model-of-the-world match) acceptable way of thinking about it, your response to that new perspective—even if accepted—will probably have little impact on you ("Yeah, I suppose you're right.") Erickson, on the other hand, wants his proffered new perspective to carry the force of a revelation, thereby insuring that (1) it will not be ignored, (2) that it will compel the individual to re-sort beliefs and experiences with respect to that new perspective, and (3) that the experience itself of acquiring that new perspective/revelation will have sufficient impact and presence to sustain itself while new behaviors are generated in response to it. Erickson accomplishes this by getting his client to commit herself to defending her own position (". . . that's your *error*. You haven't read the Song of Solomon. You SHOULD have read your bible"), then offering her a new perspective that is both reasonable and acceptable within her model of the world, and is in accord with her own wishes in terms of a desired state. The dramatic change in internal responses that occurs when the individual goes from totally defending his or her initial position to one of embracing a different perspective is what makes the maneuver an impactful intervention rather than a shrug-able attempt at reassurance. (This particular point is one of the most important to be made in this book in relation to compelling change in others, but will, however, be given only cursory treatment here in favor of a thorough presentation in a forthcoming volume on metaphors.) (The parenthetical statement just made is an example of another important pattern characteristic of Erickson's work.)

> 4. Get the individual to commit him or herself to defending his/her *present* perspective.
> *Erickson tells the fat-fannied woman that she is in "error" about her fanny being unattractive.*

The last step is, of course, to present your client with the new perspective. As stated above, the novel cause-effect relationship you generate for your client need not reflect the "real" or even believable world as you or someone else knows it. The only constraint is that it be coincident with your client's model of the world, that is that it utilize and pace that individual's own undestandings about what "is", and what is possible. (By the way, part of pacing the client's model of the world is your own congruency in stating the perspective you have generated for them. By "congruency" we mean that your voice tonality and analogue behavior, as well as the sequencing of the ideas you have been professing, all match the words you are saying. You must provide your client with the impression that YOU believe what you are saying, or run the risk of that client framing your communication as insincere and, so, ignorable.)

5. Make explicit the cause-effect relationship between the presently unwanted behavior/characteristic and the highly valued desired state you have identified as being within the client's model of the world.
Erickson describes her fat fanny as being a "wonderful cradle for children".

(This is not all there is to the intervention. You may have noticed in the case example presented above that Erickson goes on to utilize the change in perspective he has generated to engage the woman in certain kinds of behavior. This utilization will be discussed in the next chapter.)

More concisely:

1. Identify the cause-effect relationship as believed by the individual.
2. Identify some highly valued desired state or criterion with which the unwanted behavior/characteristic is (or could be) connected.
3. Pace your client's experience by explicitly stating your understanding of what he or she identifies as being the cause and effect of his/her problem situation.
4. Get the person to commit him or herself to defending his/her *present* perspective.
5. Make explicit the cause-effect relationship between the client's presently unwanted behavior/characteristic and the highly valued desired state you have identified as being within their model of the world.

Following is another example of Erickson using this same pattern with another of his clients. As you read through it, take the time to identify for yourself the elements of the algorithm we are using to describe this pattern:

A woman wrote me asking for therapy . . . I wrote back and told her I'd see her, why doesn't she call on the phone? She wrote back, "I'm too ashamed to call on the phone. I don't think you could *stand* the sight of me. I don't think you'd *stand* hearing what I have to say." Then she wrote she'd like an appointment but would I please give her an appointment well after dark and would I make *certain* that nobody saw her enter the office, or see her leave. I wrote back that I'd meet her wishes. I was really curious about a patient that fearful of seeing a doctor and so insistent. It took her about six months for her to get up enough courage to come after dark, and very reluctantly she told me her story. She was in college at ASU. She was writing on the blackboard and she passed flatus loudly, and she was so embarrassed she ran out of the room, went to her apartment, locked the door, drew down the blinds, and thereafter ordered her groceries by phone, and had her groceries dropped at a certain place where she could pick them up after dark. And she remained in her apartment six long months with the blinds *drawn*. I asked her her religion and she said she'd recently been converted to the Catholic faith. I asked her what she *knew* about passing flatus or breaking wind. She said, "It's a HORRIBLE, AWFUL thing to do . . . AND TO DO IT PUBLICLY! Other people hear it. It's just too awful!!" And she stays in her apartment for six months, ordering her food by phone and picked up after dark. I saw her a few times, always questioning her about her religious faith. And she was *really* a converted Catholic. People who convert to Catholicism are usually very, very devout. I questioned her extensively about her devotion to the Catholic Church and she avowed herself to be a TRUE Catholic . . . "It's the only true Christian faith." Then I asked her, "Who made man?" "God did." "How did He fashion man?" "After Himself." "And woman?" "He fashioned her from man's rib." "Do you ordinarily expect God to do sloppy work?" She said, "How can you speak so disrespectfully?" I said, "YOU'RE THE ONE that's disrespectful!!" She said, "I am not." I said, "I can PROVE you are." I hauled out my anatomy book, showed her the cross section of the human body at the pelvic level. I said, "You say God fashioned man after His own image. These illustrations show you in detail some of God's handiwork. I think the rectal sphincter is the most marvelous piece of engineering and I don't know any human engineer who can fashion a valve that holds solids, liquids and air and can emit *downward* just air. I think you ought to respect God's handiwork. And I want you to show some respect for God's handiwork. I want you to go back to your apartment and bake some beans flavored with garlic and onion. And get into the nude. Beans are called whistle berries in the Navy and I want you to eat plenty of whistle berries . . . I want you to make LOUD ones, *soft* ones, BIG ones, *small* ones. I want you to prance around the apartment admiring God's handi-work." She obeyed orders and went back to school after first eating whistle berries.

As with the woman with the huge fanny, Erickson refrains from reassuring this client that it is O.K. to have farted in front of others. To do so would have been destructive of rapport at that point since it would not at all have paced her personal belief to the contrary. She believes that her having farted in public makes her in some way unfit to be in public, the consequence of this belief being her reclusive behavior. Since it is certainly possible, if not likely, that she will in the future have occasion to fart again in public, it is more appropriate to alter her perspective with respect to farting rather than attempt to change the behavior itself. As in the previous case, Erickson again selected something out of the woman's model of the world about which she had very strong, highly valued feelings, which was her belief in the sanctity of God and her religion. It is important to note in this example (and in the previous case as well) that before Erickson seizes upon a valued belief or desired state to use as a catalyst he first satisfies himself that it is HIGHLY valued by his client. In the above example, Erickson made certain that that gaseous woman was sincere in her respect for God's work before passing to the next step . . . of course, she had never thought to extend those respectful feelings to her rectum until Dr. Erickson made that connection for her.

Having identified the woman's initial beliefs as to cause-effect ("farting in public makes me unfit to be in public") and a highly valued content area with which her unwanted behavior can be connected (respect for God's handiwork) Erickson goes on to get her to defend herself as one who is properly respectful of God's work. Again, polarizing her in this way serves to make the revelation of God's engineering a dramatic and powerful experience. Erickson then describes for her just how farting is a demonstration of God's handiwork, rather than the shameful lack of control she had believed it to be. For this woman the effect of this new perspective is to turn what was once an onerous breech of etiquette into an opportunity for reverence, making it in turn possible for her to engage in additional learning experiences, as directed by Erickson, and ultimately, to rejoin society.

(We would like to emphasize that this case is not merely an example of "prescribing the symptom," a sometimes useful technique of brief therapy. In prescribing the symptom the client is encouraged or instructed to continue and even amplify the unwanted behavior, rather than encouraged to foreswear or change it. When faced with a prescribed symptom the client may discontinue his inappropriate behavior because it becomes too great a burden and/or because doing something prescribed is less appealing than being contrary. In this woman's case, however, Erickson reoriented her so that her flatulence became something worthy of respect, and thereby learned to respond to it differently and control it as well. Similarly, in the case of the woman with the huge fanny Erickson does not tell her to make her hips larger but rather to use them for a cradle. He does not tell the insomniac to stay up but to use that extra time being productive.)

In this next example the pattern we have been describing is not as immediately evident or explicit as in the previous examples, yet it is there.

A mother came from Flagstaff because of surgical adhesion pains following an abdominal operation. That's easy enough to take care of that. And she mentioned that her eight year old daughter *hated* herself, *hated* her parents, *hated* her teachers, *hated* the kids, *hated* her grandparents, the neighbor, the gas station manager . . . just hated everybody. And every summer the mother tried to get her daughter to visit her grandparents in Kansas. And the eight year old just *hatefully* refused. A very MISERABLE kind of girl, so I told the mother to bring the girl down to see me. And the mother came down, came into the office . . . I asked the mother what she thought made the girl hate herself and everybody else. The mother said, "Her face is a solid freckle. And the kids call her Freckles." And I said, "All right, bring the girl in even if you have to do so forcibly." So little Ruth came in just so defiant, ready for a fight. Of course I had asked the mother a few simple questions. Ruth came stalking in defiantly and scowled. I said, "You're a thief!" She knew she wasn't. I said, "Oh yes, you steal. I know you steal . . . I have PROOF of it." And she denied that emphatically. "I have PROOF. I even know where you WERE when you stole. You listen, I'll tell you, and you'll *know* you are guilty." You can't imagine her contempt for my statements. I said, "You are in the kitchen, standing on a kitchen table, reaching up to the cookie jar for cinnamon cookies, and some cinnamon fell on your face. *Cinnamon face!*" First time Ruth knew freckles were cinnamon face. It completely reoriented her. That summer she went to visit her grandparents and had a nice time. All I did was reORIENT the situation, I didn't change it, I just reoriented it. And very few people KNOW of the importance of reorientation.

It was certainly evident to Erickson that little Ruth believed her face-full of freckles to be a blight on her appearance. Erickson accesses in her the notion that what is on her face is cinnamon, which of course is spicy and good and enjoyed by everyone, and in so doing elicted in Ruth the internal responses that go along with those attributes within the context of "freckles." We include this example of the use of this pattern as a demonstration that the pattern need not explicitly follow the "steps" outlined above. The functions that occur at each of those steps are important in making the pattern impactful, but how those functions can be made to manifest themselves within the actual interaction is unlimited. In working with Cinnamon Face, for instance, Erickson (1) identifies the operative cause-effect relationship from talking with the mother rather than with the girl herself (having freckles means being unattractive), (2) selects a desired state context out of his own knowledge of an eight-year-old's world model (cinnamon is a spice enjoyed by all), (3) paces the girl by being disparaging (her behavior with others suggests that she *expects* to be ridiculed), (4) accuses her of thievery (eliciting the response of defending herself), (5) then reveals as evidence of her theft the "cinnamon" on her face (thereby equating her "freckles" with "cinnamon"). We do suggest, however, that initially you rigorously follow the algorithm outlined above until you become facile at eliciting the necessary information and at generating novel cause-effect relationships that are both useful for, and acceptable to, your client.

Sorting for BIG Liabilities

My son, Bert, at the manly age of five . . . feeling his importance as a citizen, said, "I'm not going to eat any of THAT stuff!!" . . . referring to a bowl of spinach. And I said, "Of COURSE not. You're not old enough, not strong enough, not big enough!" Mother started protesting, "He is TOO old enough big enough strong enough." And you know on whose side Bert was . . .

In the previous section we considered the situation of an individual identifying as their "problem" some behavior or characteristic that either can't be changed (such as having freckles or farting), would not be useful to change, or would entail more time and/or effort than is available or appropriate. In such instances Erickson would typically alter the individual's perspective such that the unwanted behavior/-characteristic was left intact, but that it became a resource towards achieving some highly valued end. There are instances, however, in which it is both possible and appropriate to assist your client in altering the behavior itself, rather than accomodating his or her perspective to it. An important issue in psychotherapy is the question of who decides what a client should or should not change about him or her self. If you notice a child about to stick a bobby pin in an electric outlet there is no question about the necessity of your stepping in, in some way, to educate that child about the inadvisability of his behavior. As an adult, however, there seems to be a tacit belief that you are now educated and, with the information at you fingertips, should now be left to make your own decision about the advisability of your beliefs and behaviors. This would be ideal, but a brief survey of your acquaintances will convince you that somehow mature people sometimes behave in ways which are injurious to themselves and/or others. Sometimes a client is satisfied with the way he is even though his behavior does not harmonize with his personal needs and/or of those of others with whom he is in contact. Such discrepancies may even arise with the individual's knowledge and, perhaps, intention. His behavior is inappropriate for his surroundings or is personally limiting and he doesn't seem interested in changing. For example, a man might devoutly drink two six packs of beer each day because he thinks it is a demonstration of his virility but (1) not care that it is giving him a burgeoning belly and (2) consider it "too bad" if his wife is upset about his resulting al-choleric temperament. In other cases it may be a matter of being too deep in his own forest to be aware of just how his behavior is affecting himself and others, and where that behavior is leading. Of course, in such a case there is little or no motivation to change either.

In such situations Erickson often chooses to reorient his client in such a way that what is presently personally acceptable or at least tolerable behavior (but is nevertheless detrimental) becomes unacceptable in favor of other, more gratifying behaviors. This pattern is actually the inverse of the pattern described in the previous section. Instead of making an unwanted behavior/characteristic somehow valuable by connecting to it a highly valued desired state (as in the sorting-for-assets pattern), Erickson here is making "acceptable" behavior or characteristics unacceptable by connecting them to outcomes that are repugnant to that particular individual. For example:

> A doctor told me that six year old Billy sucked his thumb and would I come out to the house and put Billy in a trance and make him stop sucking his thumb? So I made a house call. Billy had been told that Dr. Erickson was going to come and he was going "to STOP you from sucking your thumb". And Billy was very antagonistic towards me. I turned to the doctor's wife and said,

"Now, Billy is MY patient, and Mother you are a nurse
and you know a nurse should *not interfere* with a doctor's orders. And Doctor, you're a physician and you
know you don't interfere with another doctor's patient."
They were sitting there rather startled and I said, "Billy,
I have something to say to you. Your father and mother
wanted me to come out here and put you in trance and
make you stop sucking your thumb. But Billy, EVERY six
year old boy, EVERY six year old girl is entitled to suck
their thumbs as much as they want to. Of course, the day
is COMING when you'll be a big seven year old and you
won't want to suck your thumb when you're a big kid,
seven years old. As long as you're a *little kid* and want
to suck yourself I want you to keep sucking your thumb."
Billy looked very happy—his parents rather bewildered.
Billy's birthday was coming up in less than two months
and two months is a long, long time for a six year old kid.
And Billy stopped sucking his thumb BEFORE he got to
be a big seven year old. Why shouldn't he?

It certainly would have been possible to have altered Billy's parent's perspective on his thumb-sucking such that it became acceptable to them. Given sufficient rapport and skill, you could, for example, get them to regard Billy's "insistence" on sucking his thumb as
a demonstration of his learning to assert and think for himself. But
the fact is that eventually Billy will either have to give up thumb-
sucking or face ridicule from the people with whom he comes in
contact. Erickson's choice is to therefore go for changing Billy's behavior.

As in all previously cited examples, Erickson begins by establishing
rapport. In working with Billy this takes the form of Erickson treating
Billy's parents the way Billy himself would like to respond to them,
that is, by telling them that they can't tell him what to do. Erickson
goes on to tell Billy that if he wants to suck his thumb then he is free
to do so, a proposition which certainly paces Billy's own desires. Pacing
Billy's experience in these ways quickly establishes Erickson as someone who "understands" and should be listened to. This pacing of

Billy's experience also greatly inflates his sense of conviction and security about his acceptance of his behavior. This is, of course, the set-up that makes impactful the communication that is to follow (in the same way that polarizing the client was the set-up for change in the pattern of the previous section.) Erickson then takes the wind out of Billy's sails by connecting thumb-sucking with being a "little kid." Billy is becalmed by the presupposition contained within, "As long as you're a little kid and want to suck yourself I want you to keep sucking your thumb," which, because of the legitimacy Erickson has accrued up to this point and because of the off-hand way in which it was done (that is, Erickson was apparently congruent and sincere about what he was saying), instantly created in Billy's mind an equivalence between thumb-sucking and being a little kid. Erickson's understanding of the culture of young boys allowed him to choose a context to which he knew Billy would respond—that of "size." Boys Billy's age are normally vitally concerned about successfully progressing through each age, getting older, bigger, and stronger. Ask any young child how old he is and, unless it happens to be the day of his birthday, he will tell you that he is "six and a QUARTER," or "six and a HALF," but never just "six." The idea of being considered a six year-old boy when actually seven is, of course, a detestable affront to any youngster, including Billy, who when faced with the choice allows his thumb to dry out rather than put his seven year-old status in jeopardy. Following is an algorithm describing this intervention.

The initial step in utilizing this intervention strategy is to identify just what pattern of behavior you wish to change. The specification of this behavior could come from either your client or be a consequence of your own considered judgement. As we have been describing in many different ways throughout this chapter, HOW people think about the world, themselves and their behavior can and does have a tremendous impact on their experience, both in terms of their internal responses and in terms of compelling new behaviors. This means that it is entirely possible for individuals to know that their behavior is inappropriate (or worse) and still not be thinking about that behavior in a way that COMPELS them to alter that behavior. Consider, for example, the fact that it would be practically impossible in this day and age to find a person who smokes cigarettes who does not also know that their smoking is inevitably injurious to their health. Knowing about the dangers of smoking, however, does not in and of itself prevent millions of people from smoking, while at the same time there are many others who, by virtue of how they think about themselves and smoking, have quit or who would never begin smoking in the first place. The point of this digression is to alert you to the notion that within the context of the patterns we are describing in this chapter the "reality" of the world, its laws, and your own understandings about what is right and wrong are not the useful targets of your therapeutic interventions with others. They are, rather, simply the justifications for problems.

One mother came in and said, "I'm overweight. I've got four children. I'm setting a bad example. I'm *ashamed* of myself. I'm always *too busy* to go anywhere with them. The truth is I'm too busy EATING! I keep having to go to the store to buy candy and cookies to eat—I NEVER have time to take my kids anywhere." I said, "I'm sorry for your poor kids growing up in ignorance . . . never discovering what the Botanical Gardens look like, and to never ONCE have the chance to climb Squaw Peak, never ONCE going to the Grand Canyon, never once seeing the Petrified Forest or the Painted Desert or the Meteor Crater or Casa Grande or Pueblo Grande or old Tucson. I think it's terrible to *do that* to your kids. Now go home and paste to your mirror a piece of paper that bears the wording 'Let the damn kids grow up ignorant' and leave it there. You have good reason NOT to look in the mirror. But they'll be no way for you to forget what's on that paper pasted on the mirror." Two years later she called me up. "I'm down in weight now, my kids have visited every sight in Arizona. Can I take that piece of paper off the mirror?!!" I told her she COULD take it off, but she ought to look not in the mirror but at the growth and development of her children. It took two years of practice learning to enjoy them, enjoy Arizona sights. I think that sort of treatment is much more helpful than trying to dig into a long forgotten past that CAN'T be changed.

What IS of vital importance with respect to working therapeutically with another person is the nature and consequences of the actual behaviors that that person engages in and the frame of reference (beliefs/understandings/perspectives) that make those behaviors possible. Identifying the nature and ramifications of the behaviors are important for they determine the effectiveness, competency, and quality of interactions with others that that individual enjoys (or not) throughout his or her life. The perspectives that a particular individual has are important because they constitute a malleable resource that can be transfigured in order to affect those behaviors. In working with Billy, for example, Erickson does not attack the rightness or wrongness of thumb-sucking, rather he recognizes the *usefulness* of Billy changing his behavior and then assists Billy in changing his thinking about thumb-sucking in such a way as to make it almost necessary that he stop (notice that, consistent with his emphasis on personal competence, Erickson structures his intervention so that Billy's experience is that relinquishing thumb-sucking is the product of his own thinking and efforts). As was already discussed, your clients may have an explicit idea of what they want to change in terms of their behavior. It may also be the case that your clients know explicitly what should be changed (either as a function of their own learnings or as a function of admonitions from other individuals) and not care or want to change (as did Billy), or they may not even be aware of the inappropriateness of the behavior. In these instances you must weigh your client's disinterest in changing against your own understandings about the possible consequences on their continued evolution as individuals (as did Erickson in deciding to take a hand in changing Billy's thumb-sucking behavior.) The first step in this pattern, then, is:

> 1. Identify for yourself the pattern of behavior to be changed, making sure that it can be changed AND that it is useful to do so.
> *Billy is sucking his thumb past an age at which it is socially appropriate.*

In the sorting-for-assets pattern described in the previous section, that which Erickson's client considered a hindrance or odious was connected to some highly valued desired state selected out of that person's own model of the world. This connection was done in such a way that that desired end became contingent upon the (previously) unwanted behavior. One of the things that makes that intervention work is that the desired state to which the "problem" behavior/-characterisitic is attached is one that Erickson has selected out of the client's own model of the world. The importance of this priority is no less vital to the effectiveness of the pattern we are describing here. In this intervention a behavior that is acceptable (or at least tolerable) to the individual is to be connected to a highly undesireable outcome, and if this cause-effect relationship that is being created is to be impactful the undesireable outcome that is utilized must also come from the client's model of the world. Obviously, connecting health hazards to cigarette smoking for people who care not a whit about health will not have nearly the impact on their thinking and subsequent behavior that it would if, say, they highly valued their relationship with their spouse and you connected that smoking behavior with the possible loss of that relationship.

> Now . . . a thirteen year old girl that weighs 230 pounds and she has a nine year old sister that weighs 75 pounds. She's been overweight since age two . . . obese. She also had a compulsion to follow this little sister everywhere— was afraid the sister was going to be killed. The mother is overweight but she looks slender compared to the daughter. The father looks great. And there is now a six month old baby daughter. The girl is thirteen and her parents have told her all the facts about being over-weight. Now what about dying? She knows them *all,* but you know, death never comes to OUR house . . . it is always the other fellow. And I know that any one of you could die in a traffic accident today. If you approached all the people that were going to die in traffic accidents in Arizona by January 1st and TOLD them, "by the end of the year, you'll be dead by a traffic accident", they wouldn't believe it could happen to them . . . it always happens to the OTHER fellow. Now that girl knows she *isn't* going to die. She ISN'T going to get high blood pressure. And she follows her kid sister, she's afraid something may happen to her kid sister. So you tell her, "Now you are NOT an elephant. An elephant can run

very fast. Someone who's *human and very fat,* they can't run fast. And you ought to KNOW that. And you could tire very *easily.* And your kid sister can climb a mountain much more *easily* than YOU CAN, and so you say you're WORRIED about your sister . . . I think you OUGHT to be. 'Cause you're in NO shape to look after her! You have to be able to move RAPIDLY to take care of her!'' So you approach that girl and her weight through her sister . . . and she's got plenty of ground to worry about, 'cause she *can't* be on hand to protect her sister . . . she's got to be in shape. And I gave her a specious goal—VERY specious—that will be acceptable, and when she discovers the charm of having an improved figure you make an appeal to her self image.

The thrust of the pattern we are describing here is that you are creating for your clients a cause-effect relationship (which may or may not have a basis in reality) between some inappropriate behavior of theirs and the placing in jeopordy of something they themselves highly value.

2. Identify within your client's model of the world some HIGHLY VALUED criterion, behavior, circumstance, or outcome that is or could be described as being jeopardized by his/her inappropriate behavior.
Like any young boy, Billy is concerned about the accurate recognition of his age and stature.

The elements of information you have identified in steps #1 and #2 are, of course, the basis of the new perspective you hope to instill in your client. But merely asserting to your client the contingent relationship between the two does not guarantee its impact on that person—even if the cause-effect relationship you are describing is patently true. Erickson understood that facts are rarely compelling enough to alter a person's perspective (again, witness the lack of behavioral impact on many individuals of the facts of smoking), and that in order for change to occur the proper psychological environment must first be created. As in the previous intervention pattern, Erickson creates this psychological environment by agreeing with his clients about the APPROPRIATENESS of their behavior, and does it in such a way that he simultaneously promotes rapport (by virtue of his apparent agreement with their own beliefs) and ENHANCES their confidence in their present perspective. The effect of this "set-up" is to make the subsequent CHANGE in internal state of his clients a dramatic one. It is this non-ignorable magnitude of change in internal states that compels Erickson's clients to re-sort their experiences and understandings in relation to the perspective he is offering them. For most individuals the natural response to experiencing a pendulamic shift in "internal state" (usually "feelings") is to attempt to identify what occurrence *caused* that shift, and to regard that occurrence as being somehow significant (ie. "anything so affecting must be significant").

> 3. Pace and enhance the clients' security in their acceptance of their present perspective in relation to the inappropriate behavior.
> *Erickson tells Billy that his parents can't tell him what to do and that he is "entitled to suck (his) thumb as much as (he) wants to."*

Once Erickson has assisted his client in generating a psychological environment that will maximize that person's receptivity, Erickson then makes "explicit" the connection between his/her inappropriate behavior and the jeopardy it connotes for something highly valued by the client. "Explicit" is in quotation marks to draw your attention to the point that making an idea explicit to a person is not necessarily the same thing as being ingenuous enough as to say, "This is the way it is . . ." What we mean here by explicit is that the cause-effect relationship you wish to convey is made available to the individual in a form in which he can understand—consciously or unconsciously. Of course this does not rule out a straightforward statement of "the facts" as a choice. We are, instead, alerting you to the fact that there are available to you many more and, perhaps, subtler choices with respect to getting across an idea. In working with Billy, for example, rather than saying to Billy, "If you suck your thumb you'll be considered just a little kid," Erickson imbeds the same idea as a presupposition within a sentence that on its surface is a statement of his support of Billy's position: "Of course, the day is coming when you'll be a big seven year old *(you are not now BIG)* and you won't want to suck your thumb when you're a big kid, seven years old *(seven year olds don't like thumb-sucking)"*. The tremendous advantage secured by Erickson's use of presuppositions in this case is that it both preserves rapport and avoids the possibility of generating in Billy a polarity response to a direct statement while conveying the necessary information. (There are many other possibilities for the impactful yet subtle use of language to convey information. The reader interested in cultivating this facility is strongly encouraged to obtain a copy of *Patterns of the Hypnotic Techniques of Milton H. Erickson, M.D. Vol. I,* by Bandler and Grinder, for a thorough presentation of many of the linguistic patterns possible.) The explication of the new perspective need not be verbal. Erickson was fond of setting-up experiences that were themselves capable of conveying the information.

> I told a lawyer that I wanted him to climb Squaw Peak and take his four year old son along with him. He said, "You want me to carry four year old David up the mountain?" I said, "No . . . I want you and David to climb Squaw Peak, and what YOU'RE climbing for is to get an *education* . . . and come in tomorrow and tell me about your education." He came in the next day feeling very sheepish. He said, "I *got* my education. I was pooped before I was halfway up, and David was making side trips here and side trips there and kept yelling at me 'Hurry up, Daddy, hurry up!' " I said, "In other words, haven't you been a little bit overprotective of that child?" He said, "I sure *have*. He can handle himself better than I can handle MYSELF."

The next step in the sequence, then, is:

> 4. Make "explicit" to your clients the cause-effect relationship between their present behavior and the jeopardy it creates for what you have identified as being of great value to them.
> *Erickson tells Billy that as a SIX year-old little kid he is entitled to suck his thumb.*

Concisely, then, the algorithm for reproducing this intervention is:

1. Identify for yourself the pattern of behavior to be changed, making sure that it can be changed AND that it is useful to do so.

2. Identify within your clients' model of the world some HIGHLY VALUED criterion, behavior, circumstance, or outcome that is or could be described as being jeopardized by their inappropriate behavior.

3. Pace and enhance your clients' security in their acceptance of their present perspective in relation to the inappropriate behavior.

4. Make "explicit" to your clients the cause-effect relationship between their present behavior and the jeopardy it creates for what you have identified as being of great importance to them.

As with the sorting-for-assets intervention described in the preceeding section, this intervention pattern can take many forms in actual practice. What is important is that the *kind* of information described is "gathered" and the *way* in which that information is used is preserved. Time spent rigorously following the form described above will provide you with the automatic ability to make the necessary information and utilization discriminations so that you can subsequently employ the intervention in other, perhaps subtler and more creative ways.

The first year that I taught at Wayne State Medical school some of the faculty knew me by reputation and they welcomed my joining the faculty because a medical student (a senior named Jane) had a very phenomenal record . . . she had been LATE to class, EVERY class, EVERY examination, all through high school. She was a straight "A" student . . . very brilliant. She was reprimanded, scolded, rebuked, threatened, she always apologized prettily and promised so sweetly not to be late again. That was forgotten the next day. And through high school, the perfect record of being late for everything. She went four years of college . . . *late* for every class, every examination, every lab period, and she entered medical school. She had a straight "A" average in college. She was *late* for every lecture, every laboratory period. The medical students who were her partners in the laboratory *HATED HER* tardiness . . . the professors hated it. They bawled her out, reprimanded her, rebuked her, threatened her, but YOU can't take a perfect "A" student out for being tardy who apologizes prettily and makes nice promises. But when I joined the staff I said, "When Jane enters Erickson's class . . ." and then I showed them the salaam sign known around the world, and they all looked forward happily to what would happen. Well there was no hope in reforming Jane. Now here's the auditorium, here's the door to the auditorium and here's where I stood lecturing. And the rumor before school began was passed around . . . Jane could expect something, so the students arrived to school a half an hour early—even Jane. I laughed and joked with them to the first floor, took the elevator up to the second floor, into the auditorium. At eight o'clock I began my lecture. Everybody was there except Jane. Students weren't looking at me or listening to me, they were looking at that door. And about twenty minutes late the door quietly opened. Jane slipped in so quietly . . . she had a practice of slipping in, going across the front of the room, down the far side, across the rear of the room, half way out, and back through the aisle to a middle seat. So when Jane opened the door, slipped in, they all looked at *me* and everybody knows what THIS means (he puts his finger to his lips)—keep your mouth shut. So I did this . . . (Erickson signals to rise) they all stood up and I salaamed Jane silently all the way around . . . and so did they. At the end of the hour there was a mad rush for the students to get out. They wanted to tell everybody what happened. Jane and I were the last two to leave. I talked casually about the weather and we walked down the corridor, the janitor stepped out and silently salaamed her, the secretary stepped out—salaamed her, the DEAN stepped out . . . she got salaamed all day long. She was the first student in the classroom the next morning. Three years later she came to me to discuss the effect of that one bit of therapy I did on her, yet it completely changed her way of behaving, thinking and doing.

Sorting for Relevance

The primary difference between the two intervention patterns so far described is that the first (sorting for assets) involved the creation of a cause-effect relationship between an unwanted behavior and a desired state, while the second intervention (sorting for BIG liabilities) specified the creation of a cause-effect relationship between an otherwise acceptable behavior and the loss of some highly valued state. But many more attributes are common to them both than are distinct. The succesful utilization of both interventions is based on your ability (1) to identify within your client's model of the world those highly valued content areas that will prove compelling when utilized, (2) to achieve and maintain rapport with your client (which in the interaction translates as their trusting your judgments to be credible), (3) to generate in your client the responsive environment that will make your intervention impactful, and (4) to communicate that new perspective in a way that is, to your client, sensible, congruent, and compelling.

The one additional feature that is common to both of these patterns is that it is *Erickson* who is specifying for his client the content of the appropriate change in perspective. This was by no means always the case when Erickson wished to effect a change in perspective in one of his clients. Erickson's work is full of cases in which he arranged for his clients to have some kind of experience, the intention of which was to provide those individuals with environments within which they would have the opportunity to generate for themselves a new and, hopefully, more useful way of thinking about their situation.

Now, how many things do patients have an interest in? Now the thing I do with patients is I send them to climb Squaw Peak. An example would be the married couple that came from Philadelphia. He was a psychiatrist in active psychoanalysis three times a week for thirteen years. His wife had been in active psychoanalysis for the six years of their marriage. And they STILL felt they needed more therapy. They came out and told me that much of their story. I said, "Is this you first trip west?" They said, "Yes." I said, "Being that the landscape is a lot different than Philadelphia then you ought to *discover* a few things about this world in which you *live*. So, Doctor, I will assign you to climb Squaw Peak, *alone,* this afternoon . . . you come in tomorrow and report your experience. And wife, I assign you to visit the Botanical Gardens and come in tomorrow with your husband and report upon your visit to the Botanical Gardens." And he came in and said, "You know that was the most wonderful experience I've had in life. It gives me a new perspective on life—everything looks different from the top of Squaw Peak. I never realized you could see things so differently." And the wife said, "I had the most boring thing ever happen to me, spending the whole afternoon in the Botanical Gardens . . . same old thing over and over again. It was a sheer waste of *time.*" I said, "All right. Now I'm going to assign you a different task to be done independently. Doctor YOU'LL visit the Botanical Gardens and wife you'll climb Squaw Peak and come in tomorrow and report on it." They came in and he told me what a wonderful experience it was to visit the Gardens . . . all the different plants, many varieties. "I could spend DAYS just wandering around seeing things, and I'm going to go back again." I asked the wife for her report. She said, "That stupid mountain you told me to climb . . . I cursed you every foot of the way up. I cursed MYSELF for climbing it. I swore I'd never do it *again.* I admit I had a moment of triumph when I reached the *top* . . . and I cursed you more eloquently every step of the way down. And I swore to myself I'd never, *never again* do such a foolish thing as that." And I said, "All right, now instead of assigning you tasks I'm going to suggest that each of you choose your OWN task *to perform* and come in tomorrow and report on it." They came in the next day and the Doctor said, "I went back to the Botanical Gardens. That place is fascinating. I could spend *days,* WEEKS there. It's marvelous." And the wife said with some embarrassment, "I SWORE I'd never climb that stupid mountain again, but I *did.* And I swore and swore at you all the way up. I admit I did have a momentary feeling of triumph at the top of the mountain, but I lost it and I swore and swore at you all the way down . . . I swore at myself." I said, "Fine, you've now completed your psychotherapy. Go back to the airport and return to Philadelphia." They looked at me in absolute *HORROR.* I wish I could have been on that plane and listen to what they had to say. When they reached home his wife said, "I think I'll take my car and go for a drive and clear the cobwebs out of my mind." He said, "That seems like a good idea to me . . . I'll do the same. MY mind certainly needs to be cleared up." I learned later she went to her psychoanalysist, discharged him, went to her lawyers and filed papers for divorce. He went to his psychoanalysist, discharged him. Went to his office, started putting all his records in order, tidying up his office. When he was served his divorce papers he called me up and said, "My wife is on the extension. I want you to talk her out of that silly idea she has of divorcing me." I said, "I've never discussed divorce with EITHER of you. I'm not going to take any responsibility for it *now."* She went ahead with the divorce and then she got a new job that she likes. She is enjoying life. He has a nice practice and he has a new girlfriend. She's got a new boyfriend. And they're enjoying life and both send me patients. And when they climbed Squaw Peak she experienced a momentary sense of triumph at the top. They climbed the mountain

of marital despair . . . thank God this day is over, but a
new day begins. And so that was simply symbolic psychotherapy. He got a new perspective on life. He didn't
know what he was talking about, but he spoke correctly.
She got more and more and more of the same thing over
and over again . . . she didn't know what she was talking
about, but she spoke correctly.

In the case of the Squaw Peak couple Erickson engages them in
experiences that are intended by him to provide them with new
perspectives. But how is it that tasks that are seemingly as irrelevant
to marital difficulties as climbing Squaw Peak and visiting the Botanical Gardens nevertheless prove to be impactful learning experiences?
Part of the answer resides in Erickson's use of the presuppositions of
the existing context. This couple had traveled a great distance and
were spending a considerable sum of money to work on their marital
difficulties. They would naturally assume that whatever transpired
between themselves and Erickson would be relevant to the problem
they were paying to explore. It was this presupposition, upon which
their presence in Phoenix is based, that compelled this couple to
furnish (on some level) some kind of relevancy for their field experiences. Both of them used their experiences at the Botanical Gardens
and on Squaw Peak to reorient their thinking with respect to their
marriage. The context for their experience was established by the fact
that they were in Phoenix to work on their relationship (and, surely,
dependent upon their belief that Erickson's assignments were meaningful rather than frivolous, sincere rather than exploitive). There was
no need for Erickson to assume and then specify to them the new
perspectives that each of them "should" glean from their experiences.
Instead he provided them with two different experiences and the
opportunity to utilize and generalize from those experiences within
the context already established by their presence in Phoenix.

The second part of the answer to the question about the source of
the impact of Erickson's intervention with this couple resides in the
nature of the experiences he assigned them. The fact that Erickson
leaves the couple free to generate their own understandings as a result
of their experiences does not, of course, mean that the nature of the
experiences assigned were irrelevant. The Botanical Gardens is a place
where one can wander among neatly arranged examples of the varie-

ties of thorny plants to be found in the desert, while at Squaw Peak they faced a difficult ascent which when scaled offered a new view of the desert. The experiences Erickson assigned them, then, were ones which had inherent within them certain metaphorical connotations and relationships that Erickson considered would be useful in providing additional appropriate contexts for their deliberations.

As is evident in virtually all of the case histories described in this book, Erickson's intuitions about what kind of experience would be likely to generate the learnings that were needed are phenomenal. The response of Erickson's students to his competence at knowing what experiences to go for has usually been to chalk it up to that arcane commodity know as "intuition". As a commodity it is treated by most individuals as one of those things that you get so much of and is of a certain quality . . . and that's it. You've got it or you don't. Erickson's intuitive capabilities are certainly astounding and rare, but they are not the result of a fortuitous allotment. Rather it is something that he has earned through his own (one suspects ceaseless) efforts at experimenting with people so as to make patterned sense out of the things that we all do to create our personal experiences.

When you LOOK at a problem you look at it in ALL possible *ways*. I was in Mexico City visiting a dentist there. He told me his wife was an artist. She denied it and he insisted she WAS. I thought she was self-effacing. I asked to see some of her sketches. And, she brought out her sketches . . . and there was an unusual scroll along the border of each picture. And very nice sketches of faces, flowers, animals and so on. And I picked up the picture and looked at it. I turned and looked at it this way, I looked at it this way, (turning the picture at all angles), I turned and looked at it THIS way. I took a little piece of paper and tore a hole in it about the size of my fingernail, and laid it down on the ornamental border and asked the dentist, "Look". He said, "My word, there is a FACE there." I moved it along and there was ANOTHER face. Sitting in that border were hundreds of faces in every one of her sketches. Her unconscious had put them there, I had been willing to discover them there. She is now an outstanding artist and runs an art gallery in the City of Mexico.

As a professional communicator you both consciously and unconsciously glean all kinds of information about the personal set of beliefs through which your client understands the world. These chunks of information are then mortared by you into a model of that person's world which you then use as a context within which to understand his or her problem. We don't know a set of rules for transforming these understandings into predictably appropriate and effective reorienting experiences, but we can offer you a way to train yourself to generate intuitions which make that transformation. In our experience it is not that sufficient information is missing for most clinicians in the intuitive process. What is missing is sufficient experience in discovering *patterns in the responses* of clients to the clinician's interventions. Everyone has intuitions, however some individuals' intuitions seem to be consistently more accurate than others. What we do in our training seminars, and what we suggest to you, is that you experiment with your intuitions, in the following way: On the basis of the information you have gathered about your client's world model and problem situation make a guess about what would for *that* person be a *useful* reorienting idea or experience. Create in experience or vicariously that reference experience for your client. Then either directly or indirectly *find out what was your client's response(s)*. For example, a client of ours had a very difficult time speaking with her parents, being so nervous when in conversation with them that she rarely finished speaking a sentence she had started. She was very prim and "nice", as were her parents. We suspected that if she secretly knew she had done something that her parents would find offensive she would act differently around them as a consequence of having *secretly TRANSGRESSED*. So we got her to *convincingly* call us all manner of profane and crude names. When your client then returns for his or her next appointment you find out what, if anything, transpired differently within the problem context (our client, for instance, reported that she had extended considerably the length of her visits home and rarely stopped in mid-sentence, conversing normally for minutes on end). If your intuition proved fruitful take some time to pick out for yourself just what area of your client's model of the world you were responding to. Similarly, identify what parts of your client's model you were responding to when your intuitions do not pan out, then shift to another aspect of their model and try again. In this way you will be getting the feedback you need to sharpen your intuitions. It is also often useful to take a once successful reorienting experience and try it with several different individuals. By examining your client's various responses you may then be able to identify for yourself just what are the salient features in the effective reorienting of limiting beliefs and behaviors. (We want to bring to your attention that we are not here talking about figuring out "why" people do what they do, but what CONTINGENCIES *consistently* produce what outcomes. For instance, you can know that MOVING THE SWITCH on the wall up or down will *consistently* determine the outcome of whether or not the light is on, without your having to know "why" operating the switch creates or extinguishes the light.)

Of course the ability to continually build your intuitions about the possible impacts of various experiences will be of use to you throughout your work. It is especially important in utilizing the intervention we are discussing in this section, for as was said above, even though in this intervention Erickson is leaving the explication of the new perspective up to the client, he is still exerting an important influence on the outcome by virtue of the experience he assigns or creates. Even though Erickson will not be "telling" his client what he wants him/her to know, Erickson must still consider what outcome he does want for that individual so as to have a basis from which to generate an experience that he thinks has inherent within it the lessons he hopes to convey. In the following case, for example, rather than telling the girl what experience to have, Erickson accesses a situation that gives her that experience.

> Now an eleven year old girl and her mother came to see me. As soon as I heard the word "bed wetting" I sent the mother out and took the history from the girl. She had had a bladder infection in infancy. It had persisted for years and years. She had been cystoscoped innumerable times . . . she had eventually lost a kidney before it finally cleared up. She had been cystoscoped so much her bladder sphincter had been literally *ruined.* So if she relaxed

in the daytime she'd wet her pants . . . as soon as she fell asleep her body went into relaxation, she'd wet the bed. Her parents thought, since she had been treated for the infection for several years, it was about time she developed some self control. Her sisters called her bad names, all the neighbors knew about her bed wetting. She was a very pretty blond girl . . . very attractive. All the kids at school knew about her bed wetting and the school kids are *exceedingly cruel.* So after she finished telling me her story I said, "Have you seen any other doctors for your bed wetting?" She said, "I've taken barrelsful of pills and *barrelsful* of medicine and it doesn't help." I said, "Well, I'm like other doctors, I can't help either . . . but YOU can. There's something you *know* and you *don't know* you know—as soon as you know what it is that you *don't know* you will be able to have a dry bed." She looked at me puzzled. I said, "Look at that paper weight, keep your eyes on it . . . don't move, don't talk . . . just listen to me. When you first went to school you had a lot of trouble writing letters of the alphabet . . . slowly and gradually you formed a visual mental image located permanently somewhere in your brain. And while I've been talking to you your breathing rate changed, your heart rate has changed, blood pressure has changed, the tension in your muscles has changed, your motor reflexes have changed . . . so, now, I'm going to ask you a very simple question and I want a very simple answer . . . Now here's the question: If you were sitting on the toilet in the bathroom, urinating, and a strange man poked his head in the doorway, what would you do?" She said, "I'd *freeze.*" I said, "That's right, now you know that you can STOP urinating, and if the same man moved on you'd start urinating again, and now you know you can stop it . . . just *freeze.* Now I don't expect you to have a dry bed immediately, but I wouldn't be surprised if you had at least ONE dry bed within two weeks. Getting TWO dry beds in succession is going to be *hard work,* getting THREE much harder, getting FOUR in succession is *really* difficult, and I don't think you'll have a PERMANENTLY dry bed within three months, but it would surprise me very much if you DIDN'T have a permanently dry bed within six months." About ten days later she brought a sheet as a token of her first dry bed. Six months later she was staying overnight at friends' homes, relatives, in hotels, with a permanently dry bed. I also explained to her, "Now some days you can be too busy to practice starting and stopping . . . that's all right, your body will give you plenty of opportunity to practice starting and stopping. Somedays you'll be TOO BUSY, that's all right your body will always give you plenty of opportunity. So you can look forward to a permanently dry bed I'm very certain within six months but *not* within three months." And in that one hour session with her I blew a three year psychotherapeutic case. Mark Twain says, "It ain't what we know that gives us trouble. It's what we know that ain't so that gives us trouble", to which I add, "and it's the things that we know but don't KNOW we know that gives us additional trouble."

Knowing that one SHOULD behave in a certain way ("control your urination") is different than having the experience of actually doing it (feeling her sphincters contract). In this example it is obvious that Erickson knew what new understanding he wanted the girl to have. He then utilized hypnosis to assist her in accessing in her own experience a situation that he "intuitively" knew would naturally provide her with that experience. (It is also important to notice how Erickson established rapport between himself and the girl by saying he was as helpless as all of her other unsuccessful doctors, most of whom had undoubtedly assured her that they knew what to do.) The form that this intervention takes is, simply:

1. Identify for yourself what change in perspective would be the most useful for your client (it could fall into either of the forms described in the two previous sections).

2. Generate an experience that would NATURALLY lead one to acquire that perspective.

3. Maintaining rapport at all times, assist your client in accessing that experience either through external behavior in the real world or vicariously through the utilization of internal representations.

Following is an example of Erickson using this intervention and utilizing fantasized experience to effect the necessary change in perspective. Erickson's work with this client is, to our minds, a stunning example of elegant therapy both for its economy of time and effort (on the part of the client) and for its dramatic effectiveness.

Now there is another case I think I ought to tell you about. I was asked to lecture at the Boston State Hospital at a National Psychiatric meeting, and Dr. X at Boston State was in charge of the program. And Dr. X told me he would like to have a demonstration of hypnosis . . . asked him about a subject. He said just wander around and find one. I walked around the ward . . . I saw a rather pretty nurse. You know how pretty nurses as the subject are easier to look at. And I introduced myself and asked her if she would be interested in being a subject. She said, "Yes, she WOULD be." I said there are a few preliminary tests to see how responsive she was, and I noticed she was a very capable girl. So I went and told Dr. X I had picked out Kim. He went into a state of shock. He said, "That girl has been in psychoanalysis for several years. She set the date for her termination of her job at the hospital. She had given away all her personal property, jewelry and so on . . . And she set the date for her *suicide.* You can't use HER as a subject. That girl is a suicidal patient!!" He said she was absolutely determined to commit suicide. I said, "I made an agreement with the girl. I can't BREAK it. I might precipitate suicide. I'll have to take my chances otherwise." They sought and tried to get a court injunction. The court said she was 21—I was 21—and we had our rights. It was up to us . . . he couldn't issue a court injunction. And all the doctors tried to persuade me not to stick to my statement. I told Kim I was going to be using her that afternoon. I told her where to sit in the auditorium. I lectured on hypnosis and used various other subjects demonstrating things, and then I called on Kim: "Kim, will you please come up to the stage . . . walk slowly, not too fast . . . by the time you get to the middle of the stage you'll be in a fairly deep trance, and when you get to ME you'll be in a profound somnambulistic trance." And that is exactly what happened. Well then I illustrated various hypnotic phenomena and then to illustrate a somnambulistic subject's ability to visualize and hallucinate auditorily and visually, I suggested to Kim to go to the Boston Arboretum and see all the bushes and trees, flowering plants. We had a nice walk through that Arboretum. And Kim commented freely. Then I suggested we make a trip to the Boston zoo. And Kim was very much impressed by that baby kangaroo. I knew about that baby kangaroo in advance. She looked at the tiger cubs . . . all the animals there. Then we returned to the hospital, on a hallucinatory basis, and I suggested she walk down a certain street that led to the beach, much used in Boston. Then told her to walk to the beach, look it over . . . the place for so many happy memories, and a place for many FUTURE happy memories. And she could look at the ocean and *marvel* at the vastness of the ocean . . . all the *mysteries* of the ocean. After she had enjoyed a walk along the beach I told her to return. She returned. You see, in hypnosis time distortion can occur. You can travel hundreds of miles in a second's time. So it didn't take much time to see the Arboretum or a visit to the beach. I thanked her for working with me and then I awakened her, thanked her very much for having helped me with my lecture, and said good-bye to her. Kim having disappeared that night, Dr. X and all of Kim's friends wondered what happened to Kim. A year later, no word from Kim . . . nothing at all about her. Several years passed. Now that was in 1956. In 1972 one afternoon I got a long distance phone call from Florida. And a woman's voice said, "You probally won't remember me —my name is Kim. After I left Boston State Hospital I enlisted in the Navy. I served two terms and two enlistments, traveled all around, and then I decided to live in Florida. I met a retired lieutenant colonel in the Air Force. We got married, I've got five children of school age and I'm working as a nurse. I thought you'd like to *know.*"

Well, I did!! I've had regular correspondence with Kim ever since. In Michigan I got a letter from her. One of the doctors said, "Hypnosis is a *farce* . . . it is a make believe thing", and Kim said, "I stood up to him and said, 'If it weren't for hypnosis I wouldn't be here!'" I wonder just how that therapy worked? I gave her a completely new view on life—beauty and life at the Arboretum, beauty and life at the zoo . . . a beauty of past memories and future memories at the beach, and mysteries of the ocean. Her oldest child is now sweet sixteen. Now just that one session . . . I knew what I was doing, I knew what I HOPED I was doing. I had no proof I was going to do it. Human beings being human tend to react in *patterns* and we are governed by *patterns* of behavior. And when you start a pattern of behavior they tend to follow it. You don't realize how very rigidly patterned all of us are.

CHAPTER 5

The Snowball

Behavioral Interventions

The Patterns of Behavior

Now human beings being human tend to react in patterns and to be governed by patterns of behavior. And once you've started a pattern of behavior they tend to follow it. You don't realize how very rigidly patterned all of us really are. In Fort Benning, Georgia I was there training the advanced marksmanship team for the events of the rifle team in the International Shoot. And I was dining in the mess hall with two lieutenants and several people came in and I watched one girl pick up her tray and look around the mess room for a suitable table. She walked past several tables where there were the possibility of her sitting down . . . and she sat down at a table where she could sit on the *west* side of it. I told the lieutenants, "That girl is an only child." They said, "How do you know?" "I'll tell you after you verify the fact." They went out, asked her if she were an only child . . . and she said, "yes". She wanted to know why? They said, "That doctor over there said you were." "Who is

he?" They gave her my name. "I never heard of him."
Came back . . . how did I know she was an only child?
She was looking around the restaurant looking for a table
where she could sit down and she had to find a table
where the west side of the table was available. So at
home papa sat here, mama sat here, she had to sit here.
People have many patterns in their behavior—don't try
to formulate what those patterns are. Wait and see how
they disclose themselves.

When you see a person extend his right hand towards you with the
plane of the hand perpendicular to the ground, it initiates in you a
symmetrical sequence, or "pattern," of behaviors in which you extend
your own right hand, grasp the other person's right hand, and begin
shaking it up and down. Now, shaking hands is certainly not an
example of particularly profound or complex behavior, but it IS an
example of *patterned* behavior. By patterned behavior we mean that
the shaking of hands has the quality of consistently producing a certain
kind of outcome (ie. the establishment of a certain kind of rapport).
Extending your hand, as described above, to anyone in our culture will
almost always result in the elicitation of a certain set of symmetrical
responses on the part of the other person, that of shaking your hand.
We can say, then, that this is an example of a (cultural) pattern of
behavior in that it predictably describes the outcome of a certain
behavioral sequence.

The range of experiences encompassed by patterned behavior is
really much broader and subtler than such obviously programmed
behavior as shaking hands, lighting a cigarette, braking for a red light,
and so on. Behaviors involving extensive cognitive processing and
awareness as well as more complex external behaviors (such as the
onset and progression of depression) and subtle, unconscious behaviors
(such as blinking at certain words) are just as patterned as are simple
"habits". In fact most of our behavior is highly patterned. A few
minutes consideration of your family or friends' behaviors within
similar contexts will make this evident. Take eating for example. Some
individuals consistently pre-cut their food before eating it, while others
consistently cut pieces off as they go along. Some eat quickly, others
eat slowly. Some look at the menu and select the first thing that looks

good to them, while others are unable to make a selection until the waiter actually asks for their order. The variations are obviously endless. The point is that different individuals do engage in different behaviors within similar contexts, and that most of their behaviors within a particular context will repeat each time they are once again operating within that context. That is, it is *patterned*. Extend your considerations to any context and you will discover consistencies in your own behavior and that of others that have been characteristic through time.

In most cases these patterns of behavior confer upon us the great advantage of not having to be consciously aware and directive of the steps involved in engaging in everything that we do, such as opening a door or tying shoelaces or ordering food from a menu. To consider each time just how you should open a door, tie your shoe, or select your meal would quickly become tremendously burdensome and completely inefficient (in fact, if you were very adept at generating alternative behaviors for accomplishing tasks you could end up stuck in a room starving to death with your shoe untied.) Having much of our behavior sequenced out in predetermined patterns frees us to utilize our conscious experience for other, more interesting considerations (so you can think about your date while tying your shoe, rather than about how to tie the lace.) Some of our behavioral patterns are shared cultural experiences, such as the handshake, while many more are highly personal patterns, such as always starting with the upper lip when shaving, putting on your pants before your shirt, waiting to be invited out rather than inviting others out, deferring the choice of movie to your spouse, and so on.

> And how often are marital troubles that simple. And married couples come in and tell me . . . we love each other, and enjoy sex, we want to try to go to sleep . . . every night it winds up in a bitter fight. *Every night* we want to try to go to sleep, we start fighting. And we love each other, and our sex life is good, and we fight when we go to sleep. Now what's the first thought that comes to your mind? How do they fight? I say to them, "So both of you grew up and developed the habit of sleeping on the right side of the bed, or the left side—that's why you fight

when you go to sleep, 'cause you find yourself on the
wrong side of the bed or HE does. In my own family Mike
and Archie slept together in the same bed one night and
both are right-hand-side of the bed sleepers. Oh what a
fight Mike and Archie had over trying to get comfortable.
Archie was on the right side, and MIKE was on the wrong
side, or *vice versa,* and they *couldn't* get settled.

One way to think about your client's situation is that he or she is
utilizing a pattern of behavior that is ineffective and/or inappropriate
for the context in which that pattern is used. For example, a person
whose behavior of consistently deferring decisions about movie and
restaurant selections to his spouse is appropriate within the context of
the marital relationship could find his effectiveness seriously jeopardized if he utilizes that same pattern of behavior when involved in his
company's board meetings. If he is to exert some influence on the
future of his company he must be able to voice his opinions about
where they should go with it. Similarly, a pianist who becomes so
terrified when about to step out on stage that he cannot play is
utilizing a pattern of behavior that may be useful when asked to do
something potentially physically dangerous (hang gliding without
prior training, for instance), but is inappropriate within the context of
a piano recital. We do not want to eliminate behavior, then, but
contextualize it appropriately, confining or relegating inappropriate
behaviors to their appropriate contexts, and creating or accessing from
other contexts the requisite behaviors. In terms of behavioral change,
what the board-member would want from you, his therapist, is a
change in his pattern of behavior so that within the context of board
meetings he would specify his preferences, and the pianist would want
the ability to walk out on stage and play his concert.

What, then, determines just *when* an individual will engage in
WHAT pattern of behavior? There are several ways to answer this
question. One is to say that individuals will engage in whatever patterns of behavior they were taught or learned to use when in a particular context. For example, you may have been taught as a young man
to defer to the wishes of others when decisions are at hand. Another
way to describe the systematic occurrence of behavior patterns is that
they are a logical consequence of the set of generalizations an individual characteristically operates under within a specific context. For

instance, believing that others will like you if you let them have their way is likely to be expressed in your behavior as deference to the choices of others. In the first example a person's response within a certain context is a function of the behaviors that have been shaped or installed, and, in the second, the response is a function of a set of beliefs or generalizations that have been somehow acquired. Neither description is, of course, correct—they are different sides of the same coin. When experience (either in the form of direct instruction or fortuitous circumstance) shapes your behavior with respect to a certain context, generated along with those behavioral acquisitions will be generalizations and criteria that are congruent with those behaviors. Conversely, changing your generalizations or criteria with respect to a certain context will result in behavioral modifications that are congruent with those world model changes. That is, what you believe is right, wrong, useful, not useful, fun, important or dangerous in a particular context will determine how you respond (behave) in that context.

What reference experience (criteria/beliefs/generalizations), you sort for, then, will determine to a great extent the appropriate behavior within the specified context, and it is also the case that *behavioral experiences* modify existing generalizations and/or generate new ones (via re-sorting of criteria). The domain of the previous chapter was Erickson's use of his client's perspective (ie. reference experiences) as a means of altering his or her behavior and, so, bring about change. In this chapter we will examine how Erickson utilizes his client's patterns of *behavior* as a way of usefully altering his or her perspective and, so, bring about change.

Having the ability to intervene on behalf of your clients through a utilization of their model of the world and/or through their patterns of behavior confers upon you a flexibility and thoroughness that is of obvious advantage. How, then, do you go about identifying a pattern of behavior from the wealth of behavioral and verbal information relayed to you by your client? To answer that question we first need to make a distinction between the *content* of a problem and the organization of that content into *patterns*.

Content and the Patterns of Behavior

The content of your client's problem includes the specific people and places involved, the names of the unwanted behaviors and feelings, and the names of the specific outcomes which he or she is after. Take as an example the statement, "Well, it's loneliness . . . I don't know what it is but I just don't see myself having a satisfying relationship with a woman." The content stated and implied in this person's statement includes the following: the problem is in relation to "women", he is "lonely" now, and he wants to have "a satisfying relationship". In other words, the content of a problem will be contained in the definitional meaning of the individual words used to describe it. The *patterns of behavior,* on the other hand, are what that person *consistently or characteristically does in behavior in relation to those content distinctions.* As there is no description of behavior or sequences of events in the above example (only a string of unspecified nouns and noun phrases "loneliness," "satisfying relationship," and "woman") there are no behavioral patterns to be gleaned. What is missing in the example is a description of *how specifically* he does go about generating "relationships" with women. Suppose we were to find out that, "Well, I met this woman last night and I was attracted to her, but when I went to talk with her all I could think of was whether or not I was acting right . . . I was so worried about that that I couldn't think of anything to say." This narrative gives us some information as to the sequence of behaviors involved. That is, he approaches a woman that he finds attractive, "worries" about his behavior, and is left with nothing to say. (Obviously there are still many things left unspecified, but at least we now have some information about his *sequence of behaviors* within the context of meeting women.) This is the sequence for that example, but not necessarily a pattern. If we find out that this sequence is the same whenever he attempts to meet a woman to whom he is attracted then we will have identified a pattern—a sequence of behaviors characteristic to some particular context.

As was said earlier, all behavior will be useful within SOME context, and so it becomes important to have some understanding of the contexts within which your client utilizes the behavior he wants to change. If you find it being used inappropriately in many contexts you may want to broaden the range of application of your intervention. Similarly, you would want to leave intact contexts in which your client's behavior is useful. What IS the context in our example above? "Meeting attractive women"? We might find out upon questioning him further that he goes through this sequence of behaviors when meeting ANY woman, or meeting any NEW person. If we found out that this person was also inept when presenting to his boss suggestions for changes and possibilities in the business, we could be pretty sure that the context for his pattern of behavior was not "meeting women" or "meeting new people", but the broader context of (perhaps) "trying to impress someone." The context, then, is *when* the pattern of behavior occurs, and may be in relation to "who" (Edith, secretaries, attractive women, women, anyone, etc.), "where" (home, on the bus, at work, etc.), "when" (in the morning, at 3 P.M., etc.), what "activity" (meeting people, impressing others, cooking dinner, etc.) and so on.

Although the distinction between content and patterns of behavior seems at first trivial, it is, in fact, crucial to understanding the nature of the therapeutic interventions typical to Erickson's work. Following is a case which illustrates the difference between the two and is a clear example of Erickson's ability to quickly identify and utilize those underlying patterns of behavior to effect change.

> A man about eighty pounds overweight entered and said, "I'm a retired policeman—medically retired. I drink too much, I smoke too much, eat too much . . . I have emphysema, high blood pressure. I like to go jogging, I can't . . . the best I can do is walk. Can you help me?" I said, "All right. Where do you buy your cigarettes?" He said, "There is a handy little grocery store around the corner from where I live." I said, "Who does your cooking?" He said, "I'm a bachelor . . . I usually do all my own." "And where do you shop?" "At a handy little grocery around the corner." I said, "Where do you buy your cigarettes?" "At a handy little grocery around the corner." "How do you buy your cigarettes?" "Usually three cartons at a time." "And you usually do your own cooking . . . where do you dine out?" He said, "At a very nice restaurant, around the corner." I said, "Now the liquor?" "There's a handy little liquor store around the corner." I said, "Well, you are an ex-policeman and you want to correct your blood pressure and your obesity, emphysema, and you buy your cigarettes three cartons at a time. Now your therapy isn't going to require very

much. You can do all the smoking you want . . . buy your
cigarettes one package at a time by walking to the other
side of town to get the package. As for doing your own
cooking, well you haven't much to do so shop three times
a day. Buy only enough for one meal but no left-overs.
As for dining out, there are a lot of good restaurants a mile
or two away . . . that'll give you a chance to walk. As for
your drinking . . . I see no objection to your drinking.
There are some excellent bars a mile away. Get your first
drink in one bar, your second drink in a bar a mile away.
And you'll be in excellent shape before very long." He
left the office swearing at me in the most eloquent fashion. Now why would I treat him that way? He was a
retired policeman . . . he *knew* what discipline was and
it was entirely as a matter of discipline. And there would
be no way for him to refuse from any other way. He left
swearing at me . . . he was very eloquent. About a month
later a new patient came in and said, "A friend of mine
referred me to you. My friend was a retired policeman.
He said you were the only psychiatrist who knows what
he is talking about."

In this case the ex-policeman's complaint involved several content
areas: smoking, drinking, obesity, emphysema, and blood pressure.
What is important for our purposes here is to recognize that *the
pattern of behavior that supported all of these different content areas
was the same:* whenever the ex-policeman wanted something he ob-
tained it in the way that involved the least expenditure of energy.
Finding at the content level "why" he smokes, "why" he drinks, and
"why" he overeats will almost certainly produce justifications in the
form of three additional areas of content (perhaps: "I smoke for
RELAXATION, drinking helps me forget my WIFE, and eating
helps me keep from being BORED.") Erickson realizes that the
ex-policeman's various problems are—at the pattern level—all the
same problem. Instead of dealing with the content of the ex-policeman's complaints, Erickson alters the pattern of behavior which makes
it possible for those problems to exist at all. That is, Erickson instructs

the man to satisfy his need for food, alcohol, and cigarettes in the *least* efficient way by obtaining them in their smallest units. In this way Erickson insures that the ex-policeman's intake of those abusable commodities is automatically moderated, and that he simultaneously gets the exercise he needs to retune his body. (Note that, as Erickson himself mentions, it was his utilization of the ex-policeman's disciplined background—his sub-culture—that allowed Erickson to achieve the rapport he needed to make this intervention. It was that disciplined background which assured Erickson that the retired policeman would follow such rigorous instructions. See Chapter III, Cultural Rapport.)

Instead of dealing with the content Erickson alters the supportive patterns of behavior, which ultimately results in the individual to some extent and in some way re-sorting his or her experience and criteria in relation to the specified context (that is, generates a new perspective). In our ex-policeman example, for instance, one can reasonably assume that, as a result of his new regimen, his obtaining food, alcohol, and cigarettes ultimately became the means of keeping fit, meeting people, and so on. Initiating a new pattern of behavior will almost certainly result in your encountering novel people, things, and experiences in the environment and in your having the opportunity to create new generalizations about yourself and the world.

Identifying Patterns of Behavior

People will tell you a great deal if you note their habits. At Wayne County Hospital one of my residents said, "Dr. Erickson, there is a new patient just arrived and I want you to come to D-5, and get off the elevator, and walk straight down the corridor to the nurses' station . . . and I'll be sitting in that station with my back towards you, and I want you to look right and left and find the patient that was admitted today. And then come into the nurses' station and identify him to me." I walked down the corridor, looked to my left, to my right, went to the nurses' station and said, "Louie, you're the fool. That man is standing right there at the side corridor." He said, "How do you know?" I said, "He's standing there, hands at his

side, looking straight ahead, his heels are six inches away
from the floorboard. The man has spent ten years in
prison." Louie said, "You're wrong, he spent twelve
years." People show things so easily. And most therapists
don't try to understand what their patients are showing
them with their behavior. Yet they are always communicating something and you ought to be aware of that.

Now that we have made the necessary distinctions between content
and patterns we are free to tackle the identification of those patterns.
A pattern of behavior is that sequence of behaviors that consistently
characterizes the individual's actions or responses within a specific
context. As presupposed in our definition of "behavior pattern", it is
the re-occurence of a particular sequence of internal and external
behaviors in response to a certain context that we are identifying as
being a "pattern" and of significance. (It is a pattern in that it repeats
predictably, and it is of significance in that changing that pattern will
necessarily have some impact on that person's subsequent responses
and interactions.) What we are out to identify, then, is what in this
individual's behavior is repeated in each instance of the relevent context. In other words, what's predictable about this person's behavior?
Culling patterns of behavior from the roiling mass of information your
client is apt to offer is an ability that sharpens with its own use. Later
in this section we will describe a protocol that you can use to identify
patterns and, in so doing, continually add to your "intuitive" cache of
patterns characterizing common human interactions.

What should you attend to when culling for patterns? There are
many useful distinctions to be made under the topic of pattern identification, but for our purposes here the most important is that of
sorting for *repetition,* and of the use of *contrast* as a means of accomplishing that sort. A single description of an example of your client's
problem situation will certainly give you information that you can
describe as a sequence of responses and behaviors, but you cannot be
sure that what you have described is a pattern unless you *contrast it
with at least one other example of the problem situation* in order to find
out if the sequence you have identified characterizes the second example as well. As an illustration let's use the case of Erickson's overweight
policeman and imagine that we are asking the questions. In response
to his complaint about overeating, we ask him about what he had for

dinner the previous evening. His reply is that he had ravioli "at a very nice restaurant around the corner." Now what, in terms of behavior, is the relevant (ie. pattern) information contained in his reply? We don't know. It could be the fact that he selected ravioli or it could be that the restaurant is nearby (perhaps, even, that the restaurant was "nice"). Needing another example for the purposes of comparison, we ask him about the previous day's lunch, to which he responds, "I had a salad at a nearby restaurant." With this information we begin to have the basis from which to discern patterns. At least in the two instances described so far, the ordering of starchy foods was NOT characteristic of his behavior, while the selection of a nearby restaurant *was*. We can suspect, then, that perhaps going to nearby places, within the context of obtaining food, is a pattern of behavior for this policeman. Some additional examples of his obtaining food will serve to either increase or decrease our confidence in this prediction of patterned behavior. Of course, in the case of the policeman, information about his behavior in other contexts (smoking and drinking) reveals that this pattern of behavior goes *across* contexts. Again, in extracting patterns of behavior from your client's descriptions what you are sorting for is repetition of behavior sequences within similar contexts. Following are two excellent examples of Erickson's attending to, and testing for, repetition of behavior sequences (patterns).

People are forever betraying themselves. A woman came in as a patient . . . she was sitting, like this [Erickson crosses his forearms, then locks one hand behind the other, and indicates that this was the position of the woman's legs] . . . in the office when my wife brought me out. I got into position, asked her her name and her problem, and she said, "I have an airplane phobia. I'm deathly afraid of planes and my husband is taking me abroad in September. I'm awfully afraid." I said, "Madame, I didn't see you coming in to sit down. Would you mind going in the other room, walking back, and sitting down?" She was surprised at that request. She walked into the other room, came back, and sat down. I said, "Madame, you see a psychiatrist for problems because you don't understand your problem and therefore you can't really describe it. Now . . . and you should tell your psychiatrist everything possible if he is to help you. I'm going to ask you a question . . . it isn't a nice question . . . it's an impolite question, but it is very pertinent and you need to answer it. Are you willing?" She said, "Yes." I said, "Madame, does you husband know about your love affair?" She said, "No, but how do YOU know?" How did I know? . . . Walked out of that room, came in and sat down. She sat down in a certain protective fashion. Her legs entwined . . . a very nice cover up. And I heard her say, "My husband is going to take me aBROAD and I'm afraid."

I'll give you another history. A woman came to me in Michigan and said, "I'm afraid I've got gonorrhea or syphilis. I've been sexually careless, my husband doesn't know about it. I've gone for a physical examination to twenty-six doctors, and all of them pronounce me to be in the best of health. Some even kept me in the hospital for two weeks while they did tests. But I KNOW there is something *wrong* with me. I said, "There is indeed something wrong with you . . . most people are convinced by ONE physical examination by ONE doctor. You've had twenty-six examinations, several hospitalizations, and they've all told you there is nothing wrong with you, and now you're seeing a psychiatrist. Well I can only speculate on what is wrong with you, and I'm going to ask you a very peculiar question and I want a very honest answer, even if my questions sound weird. When they all gave you a physical examination did they palpate your breast?" . . . "Yes." "At any time during the physical examination did you do any unexpected or weird thing?" . . . "I always sneeze when they touch my right breast." I said, "You sneezed when twenty-six doctors touched your right breast, and they of course withdrew their hands politely and discontinued to examine your right breast." She said, "Yes." I said, "Well, I'm going to call a downtown surgeon I know very well, going to give him your name and will ask for an immediate appointment for you. You go to his office and you hear what I say to him over the phone." I said, "Dr. Henderson, I have a patient in my office who needs her right breast examined very carefully . . . I'm not qualified to do that. She'll show up in the office, but I THINK she won't keep any further appointments with you. As soon as you examine her right breast, if you think there is anything suspicious in her right breast, don't give her a chance to go home, just take her to the hospital right away." Henderson called me after he had admitted her to the hospital, "She's got a carcinoma . . . cancer of the breast." She came out of the hospital. She said, "I don't want to mingle with society lopsided the way I am." I said, "Of course, you can be lopsided if you WANT to be. There's no law against your buying a falsie the same size as the other breast, a bra to hold it in place, and learn to elevate your left shoulder so that the increased weight of your left breast doesn't tilt you." I met her five years later . . . she said, "Which breast did I have removed?" I said, "Your shoulders are level. I don't know." How many women lose a breast and then have all kinds of humiliation 'cause they're flat chested on one side? . . . You can buy a falsie practically anywhere, I THINK!

In the first example above, Erickson observes that the woman is sitting in a way that is suggestive to him of a certain kind of protectiveness and attends to a pecularity in her intonation of "aBROAD". In order to find out whether the way she is sitting is characteristic of her behavior when talking about going aBROAD, or was simply coincidental, Erickson asks her to repeat the process of sitting down. These discriminations then become the patterned evidence from which he computes the likelihood of her having an affair. Similarly in the second example, Erickson has a notion of what is "wrong" with his client, but it is the identification of her pattern of behavior when being examined that explicates the situation. [1]

We want to bring to your attention that the case of the woman who Erickson asked to reseat herself points up an extremely important source of behavioral information, which is that while describing a problem situation your client will also be demonstrating much of his characteristic behavior within that problem context. When you match your client's words to his facial expressions, body movements, tonal shifts, and so on, you will soon discover that your client is DOING what he is talking about. In addition, the way your client enters the room, selects a chair, handles payment, and so on are all behavioral manifestations of his model of the world. These behaviors constitute information to be subsequently used or discarded depending upon the correlative patterns (repetitions) you later observe.

When your client describes an instance of his problem, identify for yourself what he did (and is doing) in terms of his behaviors—that is, *what or whom he responded to, when, where, in what way, and in what sequence?* Then ask for a description of another instance of the problem situation. With these two representations of similar problem contexts for contrast you have the opportunity to sort through the behavioral sequences described (and demonstrated in your office) for what is the same in them both. If there are discrepancies you consider worth nailing down, a lack of information you needed for your comparisons, or you want further confirmation of the PATTERN status of the characteristic behaviors you have identified, you can obtain a description of a third example for additional sorting for similarities. An aid to ferreting out this information is to first identify for yourself the beginning and the end of the behavioral sequence (that is, what happens out in the world that triggers the pattern and how does it end?) You can then work backwards and forwards between the two, filling in the details of the sequence. By giving yourself anchoring points for the beginning and end you lessen the chance of getting lost in the complexity of your client's experiences and the incompleteness and redundancy of his or her explanations. Then assist your client in recovering "missing" elements, contrasting them with the descriptions of other example problems you have been given for points of synchronicity. Once you have identified for yourself a seemingly relevant, accurate, and sequenced pattern you can take a most important step—testing. We highly recommend that you test your derived pattern for two reasons. The first is that such a demonstration will provide you with an excellent education regarding the patterned behavior of people in general. The second is that it will provide you with the opportunity to verify and, if necessary, refine your assessment.

One way to test the accuracy and pervasiveness of the pattern of behavior you have identified is to ask your client for more and more examples which you can then analyze with respect to their concordance with that pattern. But by far the best way to test your grasp is to create a behavioral demonstration within the office. Since you DO know the problem context, you can utilize your own (or someone elses) behavior to arrange a situation that CREATES that context "now", and so have the opportunity to not only find out whether or not your client responds in accordance with the pattern you have identified, but you also get a first hand BEHAVIORAL demonstration of your client responding in and to the problem context.

For example, suppose that your client complains that he can't seem to satisfy his boss at work. On the basis of his examples of this problem you identify that the contexts he is referring to all have to do with "being expected to perform", and that his pattern of behavior in response to that context is to agree to do it, worry about the quality of the final product, and then work at the task a little at a time, thereby stretching it out over time (and ultimately making it late). As a test of your identification of this context and pattern of behavior you could tell him that you wanted him to go into a trance in fifteen minutes, or take two minutes and tell you what you should know about his family history, and so on. In this way you create for this client a context that matches the one in which he claims limitations. If this person's response to these requests is to (perhaps) agree, but then take small steps towards trance and either tardily or never go into trance, and in the second example continues to intersperse over much more than two minutes "other" things you should know about his family history, then your pattern is verified and, more importantly, you have had an opportunity to observe and listen to your client responding within the problem context. If this client had NOT responded in a way that matched the pattern we had previously identified, then we have the opportunity to sort out just what was different about the situation he describes and the ones we created (from which we might discover a refinement of the significant context, a refinement of the pattern itself, or discrepancies between the client's perceptions and actual behavior within the problem context).

Such behavioral tests are not only a way of verifying your grasp of your client's patterns, but are perhaps the very best source of information about those patterns. We suggest, when making a behavioral test, that YOUR behavior be congruent with the test context you are creating for your clients so that the responses and behaviors that you elicit in your clients are in relation to that context, rather than being in relation to their knowing or thinking that they are being "put on," "put down," or "put out." AFTER you have elicited the behavioral demonstrations you needed you can then, if you wish additional information regarding your clients' internal experiences, reveal them as tests of the pattern, and then have your clients use those demonstrations as very recent and fresh examples for the identification of the internal experience information.

The guidelines for pattern identification and testing described above are generative in that, by conscientiously following those guidelines, you will be *continuously* enhancing your ability to both quickly and accurately identify those patterns of behavior which support the problems of an individual, as well as your cache of knowledge (ie. "intuitions") about behavior patterns that are common among people in general. The learning process may seem tedious at first, but step-by-step effort now will take you very far down the road later on.

I left the farm a long time ago, so did my kid sister. On the farm we ate supper, and dinner was at noon . . . the evening meal was supper. And we left the farm and lived in the cities ever since. My sister made a couple of trips around the world and dropped in to see me. I hadn't seen her for a number of years. We were talking about the various sights she encountered traveling around the world, all of a sudden my wife heard us say "supper". My wife was born in Detroit and grew up there, and my sister and I were referring to the evening meal as "supper". Long association on the farm had left its trace and meeting her evoked that pattern. And you watch people, and I wonder what their patterns are going to be . . . don't have any preconcieved idea. Look for one little bit of evidence, and another bit of evidence, pretty soon it adds up. You learn patterns by adding minimal bits of information and all observations. And when you look for a farm boy pattern of behavior you're limiting yourself. And if you look for a city boy pattern of behavior you're limiting yourself.

What Changes to Make?

Rather than going after extensive or profound changes in behavior Erickson usually prefers to initiate small behavioral changes, changes which simply (yet sufficiently) alter his client's patterns of behavior enough to achieve enduring and more useful outcomes. This approach is both justified and advisable. It is justified because experience has demonstrated that even a minor change in a behavior pattern will alter the feedforward-feedback loops between that individual's internal experience, external behavior, and the external world. Like an engine, a pattern of behavior is a calibrated, homeostatic system, and, like an engine, if one of its parts is removed or even slightly changed then the entire engine must in certain ways be re-machined to accommodate that change.

One reason making little changes is advisable is that clients will almost always find making small changes more agreeable than making larger ones. Whether conscious or unconscious of their behavior, clients often have stakes in interfering with their own progress, balking at or sabotaging their therapist's suggestions for altering the "big picture". By making his interventions at seemingly unrelated or trivial places and in innocuous ways, Erickson avoids an unproductive and unnecessary clash of wills. Also, as was mentioned in Chapter II, Erickson's emphasis on small interventions is consistent with his emphasis on assisting people towards self-sufficiency. By keeping his therapeutic role at an apparent minimum Erickson nurtures in his clients an experience of personal responsibility for the changes made (that is, he creates for them a reference experience of being competent at changing themselves).

As with so many other choices in therapy, selecting appropriate and effective behavioral interventions is a function of one's own intuitions. In using the term "intuition" we are referring to the process of unconsciously drawing upon one's store of knowledge about universal patterns of human response and behavior relevant to the "problem" context. Intuitions are neither fortuitous nor genetic in origin, but are a direct function of your ability to generate, discern, store, and retrieve when appropriate useful patterns of human behavior and experience. When you go fishing there is never a guarantee stamped on your fishing license that you will catch anything, but the practiced angler has learned over the years just *where* to drop his line and just *how* to reel in a spinner, and so is much more likely to go home carrying a limit than even a perfectly outfitted dilettante. Similarly, an attribute of an effective therapist is the ongoing ability to recognize, store, and appropriately utilize patterns with respect to the structure of human experience. When operating unconsciously (that is, without the therapist consciously recognizing that he is extrapolating from stored learnings), this attribute is known as "intuition".

We have discovered in our own development as therapists that it is important to experiment with interventions in order to acquire effective intuitions about what works and what doesn't, with whom, and in what contexts. As a skill, your intuitive abilities can be enhanced and honed. Beginning with the pattern of behavior which you want to change and your own present intuitions, determine what is the SMALLEST intervention you can make that will generate the MOST change in the desired direction. Then try it. If it is successful try the same intervention with someone else who has a similar problem. If it was not successful try making a different change in the pattern of behavior. ANY change in the pattern of behavior you make will have some effect on the outcome. That effect may or may not be sufficiently powerful to effect a pervasive and lasting change, but regardless of the intervention you make, your client will in some way respond to it, and that response will teach you something about the interaction between that intervention and the system you are working with (even "no change" is a response and, therefore, information). You can even utilize the intervention with someone whose problem context has nothing whatever to do with the one for which it was originally designed. In this way you will be tuning your intuitions to what intervention is appropriate for what pattern of behavior, with what individuals, and when, as well as providing yourself with a wellspring of behavioral material from which to draw generalizable patterns of human behavior.

Now when patients come to you they come to you because they don't know why exactly they come. They have problems . . . if they knew what they were they wouldn't have to come, and since they don't know what their problems really are they can't tell you. They can only tell you a rather confused account of what they think, and you listen with your background and you don't know what they're saying but you better know that you don't know. And then what you need to do is try to do something that induces a change in the patient—any little change. Because the patient wants a change however small, and he will accept that as a change. He won't stop to measure the extent of that change. He'll accept that as a change and then follow that change and the change will develop in accordance with his own needs. It's much like rolling a snowball down a mountain side. It starts out a small snowball, but as it rolls down it gets larger and larger . . . and starts an avalanche that fits to the shape of the mountain.

Engaging Behavior

There are several premises upon which Erickson's use of behavioral interventions is based. These include (1) the observation that because people's behaviors ARE patterned, any change in that pattern will result in new interactions and experiences, (2) the observation that patterns of behavior are soon perpetuated by the corresponding chains of environmental feedback created by those new behaviors, (3) by the notion that it is unnecessary to delve into the ontogeny of a problem in order to effect profound and lasting change, and (4) that there is a correspondence between one's model of the world and behavior such that altering one's behavior has a direct impact on the individual's experience and generalizations. If, then, you alter someone's patterns of behavior, his/her experience will necessarily be different in some ways. If that experience also proves to be more rewarding than what was previously the case, he/she will probably continue to use that behavior long enough to establish the complementary sets of external (others') and internal responses necessary to perpetuate that new behavior. The fulcrum upon which the success of such an intervention rests is, of course, engaging the client in a behavior that DOES prove to be more rewarding and sustaining. Having a client who is unhappy with his office interactions stand on his head during conversations will certainly alter his (and his co-workers') experience, but if that experience fails to be in a direction that is in accordance with his own interests (or even jeopardizes them) then he is surely—and appropriatley—not going to continue standing on his head. Erickson's ability to select appropriate behaviors is to a great extent a function of his experience with trying such behavioral interventions, and so, as was described in a previous section, is a skill acquireable by anyone willing to experiment. Now, what will utilizing all these presuppositions regarding behavioral interventions allow you to do . . . ?

Once while I was lecturing William asked me, "My mother's sister lives in Milwaukee. She is independently wealthy, very religious, she doesn't like my mother and my mother doesn't like her. She has a housekeeper come in, a maid come in every day to do the housework, the cooking, and she stays alone in that big house, goes to church, has no friends there. She just attends church and silently slips away. And she's been horribly depressed for nine months. I'm worried about her and I'd like you to stop in and do something for her. I'm the only relative she has that she likes and she can't stand me. So call on her and see what you can do." So, a depressed woman . . . I introduced myself and identified myself thoroughly . . . asked to be taken on a tour of that house. In looking around I could see she was a very wealthy woman living alone, idle, attending church but keeping to herself, and I went through the house, room after room . . . and I saw three African violets and a potting pot with a leaf in it being sprouted as a new plant. So I knew what to do for her in the way of therapy. I told her, "I want you to buy every African violet plant in view for yourself . . . those are yours. I want you to buy a couple hundred potting pots for you to sprout new African violets, and you buy a couple hundred gift pots. As soon as the sprouts are well rooted, for every birth announcement you send an African violet, for every Christening, for every engagement, for every wedding, for every sickness, for every death, every Church bazaar. And one time she had two hundred African violets . . . and if you take care of two hundred African violets you've got a days work cut out. And she became the African Violet Queen of Milwaukee with endless number of friends. Just that one little interview. I just pointed her nose in the right direction and said "giddyup." And she did all the rest of the therapy. And that's the important thing about therapy . . . you find out the potentials that are possible for your patients and then you encourage your patient to undertake them and sooner or later he'll get all wrapped up in it.

There are two features of this case that, with respect to the things we have been considering, are immediately striking. The first is that Erickson does not bother to delve into the woman's personal or psychological history, justifications for her depression and reclusiveness, or even explicitly clear with her the changes he has in mind for her. For Erickson it is in this case sufficient to understand the pattern of behavior that makes it possible for her to continue to be a recluse (avoiding interaction with others effectively precludes the opportunity for responsiveness from others), to recognize the effect that activity, purposefulness, and interactions with others can have on "depression" (anyone actively involved in purposeful endeavors that bring satisfying personal and social experiences is not likely to be depressed), and to have an understanding of what patterns of behavior are likely to lead to such activity and interactions (in this case, the giving of gifts that must be grown and cared for becomes a purposeful activity that will undoubtedly lead to reciprocal behavior on the part of others). The second striking thing about this case is that the tremendous impact that Erickson's intervention had on the Violet Lady's life was accomplished by introducing a relatively small course correction within an area of behavior in which she was already engaged—that of growing violets.

When Erickson says that he "knew what to do" it was a comment that he had gone into the future with the change in behavior he was contemplating for the Violet Lady, and in that way could predict what impact her flower-giving would have on others and, ultimately, what effect their kindled interests in her would have on HER experience. The computation involved in generating this intervention is the same as described in the previous section in relation to teaching yourself how to generate appropriate and effective behavioral interventions. It is essentially a matter of bringing to bear what you already know about patterns of personal and social interaction upon the *natural* evolution of your client from his or her present situation to one that is more satisfactory. (CAUTION—being able to successfully compute a predicted outcome is NOT a demonstration of the *validity* of that prediction; "successful" predictions are a function of one's *experience* with recognizing patterns within the relevant context.) We emphasize "natural" as it is invariably the case that when Erickson selects for his client a behavior in which to engage, it is one which is not dependent upon contrivance, coercion, or prayer for its effectiveness, but is one which exploits already existing patterns of personal and interpersonal behavior and experience and, so, is likely to lead anyone engaging in it to the same place. The contribution that is uniquely and characteristically Erickson is his utilization of existing tendencies, talents and predilections of his clients as the foundation upon which his interventions are built. It is this characteristic of Erickson's work that makes it at once consistently impactful and seemingly effortless. Accordingly, the question that you need to ask and answer for yourself when considering a behavioral intervention for your client is: What do I want the content and quality of my client's experience and behavior to be (this will, of course, be in relation to what they ask for), and what behavior and/or interactions would NATURALLY lead ANYONE into those experiences and interactions?

Obviously, successfully answering this question when generating a behavioral intervention for a particular client does not guarantee that that intervention will prove efficacious. The purpose of the question is to orient your own thinking with respect to (1) identifying specific outcomes and to (2) utilizing naturally occurring patterns of behavior. (We want to emphasize again that, regardless of what or how effective it is, your intervention will have some kind of impact on the experience and behavior of your client, and is an opportunity for you to augment your understanding of patterns of behavior.) The following case is as clear an example of Erickson's use of this computation as can be found:

Now, I did this by mail. A mother said, "My son is eighteen years old, he's in Harvard, but he has the most
vicious case of acne. And I'm an MD and I don't know
how to treat it and my son keeps picking at his face." I
said, "Well at Christmas time you can probably afford to
take him to some ski resort, a long distance from Massachusetts." She took him to Aspen, Colorado. And upon
my instructions she rented a cabin and disposed of all
mirrors. And in two weeks time his acne cleared up. He
got in a lot of skiing. He never had a chance to look in
a mirror, he never had a chance to pick at his face. It took
him two weeks to clear up. Being out in the cold and
skiing. His mother enjoyed skiing, it had been a family
sport for a long time. And acne is very much perpetuated
by mirrors. Now I could not recommend that to a boy
whose mother and he didn't know how to ski . . . but they
might like swimming. I might suggest they go to the Carib-
bean Islands and rent a cabin and go swimming and
scuba diving, snorkle diving every day, and tell the
mother to get rid of the mirrors.

Erickson has no direct contact with the boy. The success of Erickson's intervention is based solely on his utilization of naturally occurring behavior patterns. In general, his use of behavioral interventions
is described by the question, "What naturally occurring behavior can
the client be engaged in which will lead to that pattern which is most
appropriate?" Throughout his work, Erickson's behavioral interventions are characterized by his utilization of naturally occurring patterns of behavior. Consider the man (cited in Chapter III) who was
certain that he was destined to go into orbit. Erickson knew and
utilized the fact that anyone who tramps up and down mountains all
day is going to sleep soundly at night, as well as the observation
(admittedly a somewhat longer shot) that almost anyone is likely to
change his mind about a prediction, when, despite ample encourage-
ment and opportunity, it consistently fails to materialize. The basic
format for this intervention, then, is:

1. Explicitly identify for yourself the outcome for your client in terms of what behavior and/or interactions are needed within the problem context.

2. Identify for yourself a situation which NATURALLY (normally) results in *anyone* engaging in such behavior or interactions.

3. Utilize rapport and, if necessary, changes in frames of reference in order to inject your client into that situation.

There is a need to get patients doing something. I had a man come from Yuma. He was full of aches and pains and the only thing he had found to do was build a house for his wife . . . and he finally reached the stage of putting in the shelves. But when he found out how much the house cost he became depressed. He didn't want to buy any more lumber for shelves. He began driving around the neighborhood finding second hand lumber, and he had his backyard filled with lumber, second hand. And he spent most of his waking time moaning and groaning in his favorite rocking chair. Dr. Rogers of Yuma sent him up to see me. I told the man, "Certainly you ache and pain, and you might as well put that energy into positive action. I know a couple who have a nice yard. They want to plant a nice flower garden and they both work and they don't have time for the garden so you're going to work away at that flower garden until it is all ready for planting. And you'll inquire with the couple what they want planted and you'll plant it. And see to it it gets well started and you're to report for duty every day as if you were reporting to me. And each day I want you to drop by and tell me how you've performed." He planted several flower gardens in Phoenix. And he went home, he sorted out the second hand lumber and stacked it neatly. He put up shelves wherever his wife wanted them, he put up some shelves in the garage. He took daily walks, he went back to work, and he avoided that favorite rocking chair which he said would go to the Goodwill. Now making a patient do something is a very important thing.

SILK PURSES

As described in the previous chapter, new patterns of behavior can be the direct result of acquiring new frames of reference or perspectives about oneself and the world. These changes in perspective needn't be the product of any one experience, but may be a function of the fortuitous occurrence and sequence of experiences a person happens to have over time, combined with the peculiar way in which that individual makes sense out of those experiences. A college professor of one of the authors described a case that had been referred to him of a man who was for some unknown reason refusing to eat or go to the bathroom, and so had to be fed intravenously. This man was not very intelligent and barely literate, worked as a custodian, and lived alone. The story that the professor eventually pieced together was that this man, while cleaning an office at the university where he worked, happened upon an anatomy book which was open to a schematic drawing of a longitudinal cross-section of the human body showing the spinal cord flowing down from the brain into the coccyx. Some days later his boss became displeased with the man's performance of some custodial duty and said to him, "You know, you have shit for brains!" The man explained to the professor that consequently he was refraining from eating or going to the bathroom because he was already so dumb that he couldn't afford to lose any more of his brains. New behaviors, then, can be accessed as the result of a change in beliefs generated through the novel accessing of reference experiences.

The acquisition of new behaviors can also be the result of behaving itself. In examining Erickson's work it is apparent that inherent in most of his therapeutic interventions is the understanding that, given time and the opportunity to experience more satisfying patterns of behavior, people will naturally adopt those new behaviors as their own. Typically, those behaviors which at some time prove, by their owner's criteria, to be sufficiently successful prove also to be very enduring. You have only to observe the stream of people poking their fingers into public telephone coin returns for a demonstration of the persistence of even occasionally rewarding behaviors (checking the telephone coin return is almost invariably the product of one-trial learning). A behavior pattern (whether appropriate or inappropriate) is often the product of one or some successful experiences with a suggested, imposed, or accidentally occurring behavior on the part of the individual. A person who has in the past been successful at getting the attention she needed by the behavior of asking for it directly will probably continue to use that behavior (even in situations in which or with individuals for whom such direct requests are inappropriate.) Another individual who "finally" gets some needed attention by slitting his wrists is likely to make a different, but just as functional and seemingly legitimate generalization about how to go about getting attention from others. The fact is that *people usually continue to use what has worked for them in the past.* There is a certain security and economy in this in that it frees each of us from having to ponder just how to behave within each and every context in which we find ourselves. When eating soup, for instance, it is much easier to simply and automatically respond with a certain set of table manners, rather than having to consider the possibilities of slurping it up with your tongue, soaking your napkin in it then wringing it out into your mouth, pouring it down directly from the bowl, and so on.

This reliance on past successful behaviors can become a problem, however, if the behavior that was learned turns out to be generally not useful (though it was uniquely useful in the *particular situation* in which it was *initially* learned), or that it has become inappropriate over time as a result of changes in one's environment or needs. For example, the person above who slit his wrists undoubtedly found his behavior effective in gaining attention, but it is certainly not generally useful or appropriate behavior. In working with clients complaining of "problems" (that is, of behaviors that they believe prevent them from achieving some desired outcome) therapists often find themselves turning to the seductive past of their clients in order to discover the precedents for their present behaviors and, perhaps, the justifications for them. As described in the previous chapter there is, of course, a cybernetic relationship between one's behavior and the justifications (perspectives) for that behavior, such that altering one's perspective will in some way effect changes in behavior. Erickson recognized that a *cybernetic* system cuts both ways—changes in behavior can also effect changes in perspective.

I had a patient come to me in about March. A young girl
. . . her hair was full of snarls, her dress had tears in it,
in her hair a number of safety pins, her stockings were
wrinkled, and she said, "I'm depressed. I've got a good
job. I don't think anybody can like me. And I decided I'm
going to try psychotherapy but I know it ISN'T going to
work but I'm going to try it for several months and here's
the cash to pay you for it. That will *force* me to use all
the psychotherapy from March till August." And she *be-
moaned* her unhappy state: she had a good job as a
stenographer, and there were several young men on the
floor where she worked, and whenever she went to take
a drink several men also suffered from acute thirst which
she always avoided. One of her defects was she had a
part between her teeth, and she told me she was absolutely going to commit suicide in August. And I said, well,
she ought to have at least one GOOD memory before she
committed suicide, "So why not really play some prank
on somebody?" I persuaded her that what she ought to
do is go to the water cooler, take a mouthful of water, and
when the young man approached her she should squirt
him with water. She said, "That won't do any good." I
said, "No, but it'll be a nice memory to carry to your
grave." So she took me at my word. And the next day she
went to the water cooler, took a big mouthful of water,
and a young man she really liked but she knew would
have no interest in her, approached and she sprayed him!
He was startled and the consequences were expectable
. . . he says, "You little bitch, I'm going to KISS you for
that!" She turned and ran and he ran after her caught her
. . . two months later they were married. She sent me a
number of patients. To argue with her about NOT committing suicide would have been fatal . . . why not have
a good memory to take to your grave with you? So she
did! She is the mother of teenage children now and en-

> joying life. Therapy consists of altering the total life situa-
> tion and reactions and behavior and the interpretations.

As a first approximation of what Erickson did with the woman in this case we can say that he got her to engage in behavior that altered her interactions with the world such that she no longer considered suicide necessary. Once established, behavioral patterns are inherently enduring because of their self-reinforcing systematic interaction with the environment and the individual's experience. In other words, behaving in a certain way will net you certain corresponding responses from the world and certain corresponding experiences for yourself, so that your internal and external environment become supportive of that behavior. If you behave as though you should be kicked then some people will (appropriately) kick you, which experience in turn reinforces your belief that you should be kicked, etc. If this kickee were our client and this was Chapter IV we would intervene by changing this poor soul's perspective such that he no longer believed he deserved the boot. In the case cited above, for instance, the woman believes that she is not attractive, which belief manifests itself in behavior as not bothering to attend to her physical appearance and avoiding contact with men. Being unkempt and shunning men will, of course, preclude to a great extent the POSSIBILITY of a man finding her attractive, which then serves to confirm, for her, her belief in her unattractiveness. Erickson could have attempted to alter her perspective such that she became convinced that she was in fact attractive, which would then result in her effecting different and, presumably, more appropriate behaviors. (This was, in fact, his approach in working with another woman who was overweight and unkempt. After spending a session fidgeting and obviously avoiding looking at this particular woman, Erickson "confessed" to her that he could not continue as her therapist as he found her so attractive that he could not concentrate. The consequence of this woman believing herself to be attractive was that she lost weight and became well-groomed.) Instead Erickson arranges for her to engage in behavior (spitting water on a workmate) that results in her having experiences that decisively alter her perspective of the world and her place in it. Now merely telling a suicidal person to go spit water on someone is not likely to consistently result in a return to optimism and marriage, so let's consider in more detail the sequence Erickson employs in working with this woman.

As always, fundamental to Erickson's work is his ability to elicit and utilize rapport. His client in this case is convinced that she is unlikeable and that she must commit suicide. Instead of attempting to convince her that she is "actually" attractive and that life is worth living, or even trying to dissuade her from suicide, Erickson accepts her determination to commit suicide AND makes it an opportunity to have "at least one good memory before she commits suicide." (Remember that rapport is not a function of empathy or sympathy but of pacing, and that it is not measured by mutual affection but by trust and credibility.) Erickson's integration of pacing of the woman's model of the world (rapport) and use of that model to create an "opportunity" where none previously existed (changing perspective) is an excellent example of the simultaneity of the patterns we have been describing. As Erickson himself says, arguing with her about her beliefs would be useless (or worse) as it would only serve to polarize her position (no one likes to admit he or she is wrong) and jeopardize rapport between them. Erickson's proposition to her not only matches her own belief in the inevitability of suicide, but paces her desire to have pleasant experiences as well (if she didn't care whether or not she had "good" experiences she wouldn't be committing suicide to gain relief from depression, not being liked, and so on.) The prospect of a "good" experience is naturally in accord with her own wishes, and at the same time significantly alters her perspective such that she becomes engaged in considering how to best use this opportunity. It is this evolution of her situation into just such an (as yet undefined) opportunity that provides Erickson himself with the opportunity and flexibility necessary to engage her in some kind of impactful behavior. Except for consideration of possible methods, committing suicide is a yes-no proposition. As a focal point for discussion the act of suicide provides the therapist with little or no flexibility, only the choice to convince the individual that it is or is not the thing to do. Having a "good experience to remember", however, could mean almost anything in terms of behavior.

What it means for the woman in this case is squirting water on one of her workmates. Obviously, Erickson's choice of behavior for her is far from random. She tells Erickson that she is unlikeable and does not interact with men she is attracted to, which is certainly ample reason to be depressed. Given this situation, Erickson selects as a behavior for her one that will (hopefully) provide her with the opportunity to discover that she was wrong about her attractiveness and that interacting with men can be pleasant and rewarding. Erickson also utilizes as the instrument for effecting this experience one of the attributes she identified as being a defect—the gap between her teeth. In this way Erickson is engaging her in behavior that will make it possible for her to reorient her thinking (and, consequently, her subsequent behavior) with respect to what she considers to be her "defects." The gap between her teeth becomes the agent of achieving her desired outcomes, rather than the subverter of them. This pattern is obviously analogous to the sorting-for-assets pattern described in Chapter IV. What Erickson does here is take something that she considers to be a hindrance to her achieving her desire to be attractive and make it a part of the behavior that is RESPONSIBLE for her achieving that desire. In this way the hindrance becomes an asset. The successful utilization of this intervention, then, depends upon (1) your ability to establish and maintain rapport so that your client will be amenable to the things you have to say and suggest, (2) if necessary, your ability to alter your client's perspective so as to provide yourself with the flexibility you need to get him/her to engage in new behaviors or the behaviors that you direct, and (3) your ability to generate for your client a behavior that will ultimately make it possible for him/her to get where he/she wants or needs to go. Creating and utilizing rapport and perspectives were, of course, the topics of Chapters III and IV (although we will certainly continue to identify and discuss their occurrence and importance in all of Erickson's work.) Together they constitute the factors that will make it possible for you to actually get your client to engage in whatever behavior it is that you have determined will be useful. How, then, do you determine just what that behavior is?

As was said above, it is obvious that Erickson does not choose just any behavior hoping that by "mixing things up" they will somehow eventually coalesce into a more satisfactory configuration. Rather, there is a definite relationship between the behavior he selects and the desired outcome, a relationship that results in the seemingly inevitable triggering of a logical sequence from the one to the other. Let's consider, now, a computational sequence that will make it possible for you to generate for your client behaviors that will be similarly capable of initiating impactful learning experiences.

As has already been described, an individual's behavior within a particular context both indicates the content and perpetuates (by determining the type and form of interactions that are engaged in) the existence of that person's model of the world. And, of course, the inverse is true, such that the content of one's frame of reference will compel certain kinds of behaviors and forms of interaction. Ignoring the chicken-or-egg controversy for the moment, it is sufficient to note that behaving can lead to the solidification of a perspective that perpetuates that behavior, and that altering one's perspective can lead to the accessing and perpetuation of (contextually) new behaviors. Behaviors provide the range of ways of being impactful upon the world, while one's perspective is what organizes those behaviors according to what will be used when, where, with whom, and in what way. In this sense it is the model of the world that provides the stability and congruency over time that we recognize as characterizing a particular individual. Altering an individual's behavior, then, is significant in terms of changing that person only insofar as engaging in that behavior results in a corresponding change in that person's model of the world, for it is that change that will ensure the perpetuity of the new ways of interacting within that context.

The double question for you as a therapist becomes: What new belief/perspective do I want this person to have, and Will that belief naturally elicit the kind of behavior(s) that are appropriate and necessary? In teaching this and similar patterns to participants in our seminars we have discovered that the single most significant factor in the effective utilization of these patterns is an individual's ability to exploit the existence of naturally occurring behavioral and experiential sequences. When considering for a client some kind of behavioral intervention, most therapists jump immediately to considerations of various types of behaviors that SHOULD be engaged in within the "problem" context. The behaviors that a therapist comes up with in this way may certainly be useful behaviors to have, but their innate virtues do not necessarily insure that the CLIENT will have the same satisfying experience that the therapist has had when using them, or that he will learn the things he needs to learn from that experience. It is extremely unlikely that someone attempting to come up with a useful behavior for the suicidal woman of our example would have generated as a suggestion to "go spit water on a workmate" unless that therapist had first retraced the probable chain of cause-effect events from the desired outcome (that is, the change in perspective and its attendant behaviors) to its antecedents. In other words, the behavior in which you engage your client must be in relation to the outcome you and your client are after, such that that behavior will *naturally and inevitably lead to that outcome.* The first piece of information you need to specify for yourself, then, is, "What is the behavior I want my client to have within the identified context and what belief or perspective naturally presupposes that behavior? So . . .

> 1. Specify for yourself what would constitute appropriate behavior within the problem context and what change in perspective would naturally produce that behavior.
> *In our example above, Erickson wants the woman to interact with men, the change in perspective being her considering herself to be attractive.*

We have now identified where it is we want to end up in terms of an outcome for the client. But how is this new perspective to be generated? Consider for a moment the last time you changed your ideas about the way the world is. The vehicle for that change was either some novel juxtaposition of ideas that impacted you in a way that resulted in your amending your model of the world (this was the province of Chapter IV), or you were involved in some kind of interactive experience which was sufficiently intense, repetitive, and/or rewarding to formulate a new generalization with respect to that experience. As this chapter is about Erickson's use of behavioral interventions, it is the second form that we are interested in here. The next step back down the chain that leads to the change in perspective we are after with our client is that experience that is instructive of their intended perspective. Your client, like everyone else, will (it is hoped) alter his or her thinking in response to having a sufficiently impressive experience in the world. And, of course, as the agent of change you want to make it possible for your clients to have *that* experience which will provide them with the opportunity to learn what it is they need to learn with respect to their understandings about, and functioning in, the problem context. So the next step is to identify what experience (in the external world) would NATURALLY provide ANYONE with the learning you wish your client to have. Since you can't determine or take control over just what kind of sense your clients will make out of their experience it is important that the experience you choose to provide them be one that has inherent within it the learning you are after. By generating the nature of this experience in relation to "anyone" you maximize the possibility of coming up with one that will prove to be universal in its effect, rather than idiosyncratic. This computation identifies for you the kind of experience you want to create for your client.

2. Identify for yourself what real-world experience would naturally install in almost any individual the belief or perspective you want your client to have.
Being congruently responded to as though she was attractive when such attention was unexpected (that is, there was no apparent ulterior motive for the response) is likely to convince her that at least that particular person finds her attractive.

It is at this point that we can address the question, "Why bother to go through the rigmarole of setting up an experience for the client when he or she could simply be told what he/she needs to know?" Obviously, Erickson could have just as easily told this woman, "That those men at work try to join you at the water cooler is a demonstration that you are attractive to them, and they would tell you so under the right conditions." But often people find their experience to be profoundly more convincing than what they are being told. Witness the millions of fingers that have been tinted in the compelling quest to test the veracity of WET PAINT signs. So the first point to be made about this intervention is the fact that it provides the client with a real world experience, whose lessons, because of their "reality", are lent a credibility that is difficult to refute or ignore.

The second point we wish to draw your attention to is that in his work with the suicidal woman, Erickson does NOT indicate to her what it is that she is to learn from her experience. In fact, he leads her to believe that the purpose of her behavior is to provide herself with "one good memory". This is a very important point in terms of making this intervention effective, as it makes it possible for the client to evaluate his or her experience within the frame that it was "real" rather than contrived or a function of the therapist's "suggestions". In other words, the fact that the results of the experience were neither PREDICTED nor EXPECTED makes it possible for the client to trust that experience as a genuine representation of "reality." You will find throughout Erickson's therapeutic work this pattern of letting clients think they are in for a certain experience, when in fact he has arranged for them to undergo something quite different.

Now that we have identified what experience we want the individual to have, we have to determine what conditions would naturally lead to it. That is, what do we have to get our client to do in order to precipitate the experience we want him to have? This involves another step back in time in which you are identifying for yourself what behavior your client would have to engage in in to create the situation you are after. In selecting this behavior Erickson typically utilizes that characteristic or behavior that the client believes to be the problem. It is these "defects" and "deficiencies" that individuals rely on to justify the existence and persistence of their problem. By making that "cause" the "effector" of some highly valued outcome Erickson effectively changes his client's response to it. In the case of the suicidal woman she originally saw the gap between her teeth as an unattractive deformity. Now, of course, using that gap to spit water on her future husband may not have resulted in her becoming enthralled with the beauty of her teeth, but in the future her noticing that gap will certainly access memories of the important (and humorous) role it played in changing her life.

> 3. Identify for yourself what behavior you could engage your client in that would naturally foment the previously identified experience AND, if possible, utilize as a catalyst that characteristic or behavior that the client identifies as being the "cause" of the problem.
> *Erickson has the woman use the gap in her teeth to spit water on a young man at work.*

By working backwards from the outcome you're after through a naturally occurring sequence of antecedents you will have created a chain of effects that is likely, when set in motion, to culminate in the outcome you are after. Specifically, you will have generated a behavior that, if engaged in by your client, will lead that person into an experience that will probably instill in him or her the new perspective that you intend. Two of the factors that make this work are that perspective, experience, and behavior are contingent upon one another such that the intended sequence does occur, and that the experience that your client has is unexpected so as to maintain its credibility and, so, its punch.

Of course, once you have gathered the information you need in order to generate the causal sequence we are describing you must then get your client to actually engage in the behavior. Erickson does this by maintaining rapport (so as to maintain his credibility), and by utilizing the sorting-for-assets pattern of the previous chapter to build whatever bridges (no matter how spurious in reality) he requires between the present problem situation and the behavior he wants the client to employ. For the man in Chapter III who was "destined" to go into orbit the hikes up into the mountains were to make lift-off *easy*, NOT to prove that he was wrong. More concisely then,

1. Specify for yourself what would constitute appropriate behavior within the problem context and what change in perspective would naturally produce that behavior.

2. Identify for yourself what real-world experience would naturally install in almost any individual the belief or perspective you want your client to have.

3. Identify for yourself what behavior you could engage your client in that would naturally foment the previously identified experience AND, if possible, utilize as a catalyst that characteristic or behavior that the client identifies as being the "cause" of the problem.

4. Utilize rapport and any necessary reference frame shifts to motivate your client to engage in the behavior.

We do not know that Erickson himself goes through the set of computations that we have just outlined for you, only that he is consistently able to generate behavioral interventions for his clients that do create learning experiences that in turn have a lasting effect on both their orientation and behavior. Erickson's intuitions in this regard are consistently appropriate and effective, but, as we stated earlier, those intuitions are, to a great extent, a function of his experience in discovering what works. Using the computational sequence outlined above will not only maximize the possibility of generating behavioral interventions that are compelling, but will provide you with the experiences you need to develop your own intuitions. Following is another example of Erickson utilizing in behavior what his client considers a liability as the means by which he is led into having an important learning experience.

A couple of years ago I got a Christmas card, it said, "I want to thank you for that *excellent* time I spent with you in 1959. I know I should have written before . . . I kept putting it off. Now, I spent *three hours* with you and life has been *glorious* ever since." He was a very wealthy man. He had been trained as a concert pianist. He had

a private auditorium of his own and the first public concert he gave, or rather he WANTED to give, he got stage
fright and was unable to walk out on the stage. And while
he was here in those three hours in 1959 I explained to
him . . . oh, he had kept on practicing the piano. In all
the ten years having elapsed since the first attempted
public concert he managed to allow ONE friend to be
present in the auditorium. He couldn't stand to have
TWO of his friends to be an audience. And when he
came to me I said, "Well, your problem is very simple.
I want you to buy a stack of colored towels . . . red, green,
blue, purple, flowered and so on. When you get home
you very carefully spread them out across the stage floor,
and save the last two for the piano seat and the last towel
you put on top of the piano. Then you send out invitations
for a piano concert and have the entire auditorium filled.
And when it comes time to go out on stage you stop and
look at the first towel . . . do you want to FAINT on that
one, or would you prefer to faint on the second one?" So
he moved down to the second and had the same debate
—should I faint on this one or on the third? He got to the
piano bench . . . he knew it would be very awkward to
FAINT on it, so he SAT on it. And he considered fainting
on top of the piano, but didn't see his way clear. So he
played his concert. Now I think that is *therapy* because
it took ALL his fears and anxieties and put them in a
concrete *form* and located them on a *towel* and it was
a matter of WHICH towel. And he went down the row
of towels and each one he passed over . . . he HAD to
play, he COULDN'T use the towels. He's been playing as
a concert pianist ever since.

The pianist in this case example needed to have the experience of
successfully going out on stage and playing his concert, an experience
which would not only demonstrate to him that he had the ability to

perform in front of others, but would also provide him with the opportunity to have that behavior reinforced by the consequent applause and admiration from his audience. In this way his behavior and the environment will have conspired to inculcate him with the frame of reference that he is both capable of performing and that performing is a gratifying experience. These views (plus the inevitably resulting behavior of actually performing) become the desired outcome, with successfully giving a concert an obvious choice for an experience capable of instilling those new perspectives. The interesting question, the one the pianist himself had been wrestling with for ten years, is that of how to get him out on stage so that he CAN perform.

As in the previous example of this behavioral intervention pattern, Erickson utilizes as the vehicle for bringing about the desired outcome the very attribute the pianist considers to be the cause of his difficulties —his concern with fainting. In working with the suicidal girl, Erickson enlisted her cooperation in the behavior he had planned for her by introducing the notion of taking one good memory with her to the other side. Similarly, Erickson, in this second case, refrains from trying to change the pianist's mind about the necessity, usefulness, or probability of his actually fainting. Instead Erickson introduces the notion of fainting on the "right" towel. Notice that by introducing this consideration, the fainting of the pianist is taken for granted and, so, it immediately becomes a side (if not nonexistent) issue, having been supplanted by the more pressing concern of determining just which towel is the "right" one. What makes it possible for this change in priorities to be effective in getting the pianist out to his piano is that the set of criteria that he will use to evaluate the relative fainting merits of the different towels will be very different than those he had previously applied when considering walking out on stage. The context of " walking out on stage" meant considering such emotional and history laden considerations as his preparedness for the concert, the importance of sufficiently entertaining the audience, the reflection on his training by the response he receives from them, perhaps his value as an individual, and so on. With the exception of considering the painful merits of fainting on the piano bench or the piano itself, the selection of a proper fainting towel is a context for which he has never been tutored as to the appropriate criteria to use. Without such criteria he will be free to be concerned, but will have no way to resolve the problem (and so faint), and will therefore ponder his way from towel to towel. To recap, then, Erickson utilizes the pianist's preoccupation with fainting by making him preoccupied with the selection of the "right" towel to faint on. Not having the criteria necessary to make that determination, the pianist found himself out at his piano where, unable to faint, he played and so had the experience he needed to learn that he was capable of doing it. Even if when waiting in the wings for future concerts it occurred to him to worry about fainting, he would also access the (perhaps humorous) memory of having successfully performed before despite those same fears (ie., a reference experience for success will have been created).

The points we feel most important to note at this juncture with respect to this pattern of Erickson's use of behavioral interventions are that (1) he utilizes naturally occurring sequences of behaviors, experiential situations, and patterns of generalizing as the source of his definition of interventive behaviors for his clients, (2) rather than argue about the merits of his clients' present perspective and behaviors or explicitly identifying what they SHOULD believe and do, Erickson allows them to make the discovery on their own as a function of their own efforts and internal computations, and (3) Erickson utilizes those attributes that clients think are stumbling blocks as the kick in the pants that gets them headed off down a new road. It is this utilization of your client's model of the world and naturally occurring chains of events (most easily accessible, we feel, through the sequence described above) that will make it possible for you to eventually reproduce in your own work this pattern.

SOW'S EARS

One of my daughters came home from school, she said, "Daddy, I'm going to bite my fingernails. All the other girls at school bite THEIR fingernails, and I'm going to be in style too." I said, "Well the other girls have a big start on you. You'll have to do a lot of work to catch up with them. So why not, twice a day, for fifteen minutes at a time, you sit down and chew away at your fingernails, get caught up with the other girls." She said, "Fifteen minutes is not long enough, I'll need at least a half an hour." I said, "I think fifteen minutes is enough." She said, "No, I'm going to do it for half an hour." So I said, "I'll furnish the clock and you can time yourself." Then one day she announced, "I'm going to start a new style at school . . . NOT biting fingernails." That was very agreeable to me.

There is no need for a lengthy preparation for this next pattern, for it breaks no new ground in terms of formal patterns (even the seed to be cast is the same.) The difference is only in the method of planting. As you may have already guessed, just as the perspective-altering sorting-for-assets intervention pattern (Chapter IV) had its behavioral analogue in the pattern described in the previous section, so does the sorting-for-BIG-liabilities pattern have its counterpart in Erickson's behavioral intervention repertoire. (In fact, since words are simply a way of identifying or "tagging" particular behaviors and their attendant internal states, any verbally executed intervention should be capable of being carried out behaviorally as well.) That intervention involved the associating of the client's unwanted or inappropriate behavior with the "realization" that that behavior significantly jeopardized something he/she highly valued. In this way, what was previously acceptable behavior to his clients became associated with sufficient discomfort over impending loss to compel them to change. Instead of using the currency of verbally expressed ideas, in the intervention to be described here Erickson makes his client's inappropriate behavior decisively uncomfortable for him or her by attaching to it some other behavior, the price of which proves to be too high.

In searching through examples of Erickson's work it seems to be the case that the behavioral intervention we are describing in this section is most often utilized in working with someone who is hindered by inappropriate compulsive behaviors, such as handwashing, nailbiting, insomnia, and so on. Erickson's orientation in working with these kinds of problems is that such behaviors are inappropriate and obsolete learnings that are in need of revision. On the other hand, the most prevalent response of practicing therapists to such compulsive behaviors is that they are behavioral manifestations—symptoms—of underlying psychological problems. The usual *ergo* of those operating out of this historical viewpoint is that the individual's psycholgical problems must be examined and resolved in order to effect lasting relief from the symptomatic behavior. Erickson prefers to think about such behaviors as behavior patterns which served some useful purpose at one time, but which now persist more out of habit than out of function. Erickson's model makes it unnecessary to know the origin and significance of the behavior—it is sufficient to simply alter in some useful way the inappropriate behavior itself. Accordingly, Erickson prefers to take direct steps to alleviate the compulsive behavior itself, trusting that once relieved of that burden the individual will be free to finish therapy on his or her own through adjusting to the lightened and different load.

> Now who NEEDS symptoms? Symptom substitution
> . . . Oh, that's a nice superstition, that's really a nice one.
> If you break your leg and then put it in a cast to heal do
> you have to break your arm? If you get that corrected
> then do you have to have your ribs broken? Who NEEDS
> symptoms? You go along with the behavior but you make
> the patient wish, "I don't want this behavior." And you
> make most progress that way. You see, the past is un-
> changeable. You can discuss it endless ways and you get
> nowhere.

As is characteristic of all of his work, Erickson never attempts to directly compel his client to abandon compulsive behavior. Instead Erickson accepts that behavior and then somehow utilizes the behavior itself as the catalyst for its own subsequent disintegration, as he does in the following case:

> SOME neurotic patients . . . you have them *purposely,*
> *intentionally* do a neurotic thing. I'm thinking of a
> woman who came to me and said, "I pull out my hair.
> I LOOK at my scalp, there are bald spots. And I KNOW
> I keep on pulling out my hair—a few hairs at a time." I
> told her I could correct that for her "ONLY YOU WON'T
> LIKE *MY* remedy. I want you to give it a trial for thirty
> *days* . . . Pull out ONE hair, just one, and wind it VERY
> carefully around a match stick. Make certain you wind it
> in a *neat* coil. One hair each day . . . And try to select
> the *longest* hair." She got SO sick and tired of pulling out

just one hair she asked me if she would have to continue
that. I said, "You CAN continue by pulling out two hairs,
three hairs, and winding them separately around match
sticks." She said, "I don't want anything to *do* with my
hair!" I said, "You'll COMB it and when you take the
loose hairs off the comb, *wind* them on a match stick."
It didn't take very long for her to stop pulling out her hair,
and she'd use that *comb* and wind THAT hair 'till she got
sick and tired of it and didn't want to do THAT any more.
I had her under the obligation to find something she'd
liked to *replace* that. How many patients try to frustrate
you by doing perverse things . . . really perverse things?
And they expect you to reprove them, and you'd better
turn it around, and make them *wish* they hadn't done it.
That is you maintain your OWN integrity and give THAT
person a chance to discover his own integrity.

As in all of Erickson's work described thus far, the ability to achieve
rapport continues to be fundamental to the success of his interventions. In telling the hair-pulling woman that he "could correct that for
her 'ONLY YOU WON'T LIKE *MY* remedy,' " Erickson paces both
the woman's hope that he can help her AND demonstrates his awareness of her probable predisposition to reject the suggestions of others
as somehow unacceptable. It must be remembered that before going
to Dr. Erickson she had certainly already exhausted many, if not all,
of the avenues of relief with which she was acquainted, and so has a
history of failure and consequent "justifiable" reservations upon which
to draw when evaluating Erickson's suggestions. By pacing this predisposition of hers Erickson helps to insure that she will regard him as
someone who "understands" and is therefore to be listened to. (We
would also like to point out to you the implication Erickson creates
for the woman when he tonally empahsizes *"my"* in, "ONLY YOU
WON'T LIKE *MY* remedy." By emphasizing that it is *his* remedy
she won't like Erickson implies that there is someone *else's* remedy
that she WILL like . . . *hers*, naturally.) The other way in which
Erickson establishes rapport with this woman is by accepting—at least
in his external communications—the woman's compulsive behavior.

Again, in order to understand the significance of this seemingly sim-ple, but important, step you must consider the predisposition of clients in relation to their previous experiences. The woman in our example has undoubtedly been pleaded with and prodded by friends, physi-cians, and, most incessantly, by herself about the inappropriateness of what she is doing to her hair. And yet, despite her knowing that she should stop and trying what she and others know to do to get her to stop pulling her hair, she continues to do it. For a therapist to then tell her to try once again to change that behavior is to make her mistrustful and overly circumspect, for it flies in the face of her personal experience. By letting the behavior itself temporarily stand Erickson at least avoids the possibility of doing battle with her over the content of her past experiences, and perhaps conveys to her that he has an appreciation of just how compelling and recalcitrant a behavior her hair-pulling is (which certainly matches her experience and, so, builds rapport).

Having established rapport, Erickson allows her to continue with her compulsive behavior but adds to that behavior a rider that he suspects will prove so tedious and burdensome that she will be com-pelled to give up hair pulling. The importance of this additional behavior is that in the client's mind it is handcuffed to the compulsive behavior, so that stopping one means stopping them both. The effec-tiveness of this intervention, then, lies in your ability to (1) secure and maintain rapport so that your prescription of behavioral additions is taken seriously, and (2) in your selection of an appropriate yet ulti-mately burdensome behavior to prescribe. The appropriateness of the assigned behavior refers to the notion that that behavior makes some kind of sense to the client in terms of its relevence to the problem situation. Although it may be burdensome to have to walk backwards every other hour, prescribing that as an adjunctive behavior to the hairpulling woman or Erickson's daughter will only serve to generate in them doubt as to the competency and altruism of the therapist. The story about Erickson's daughter that opened this section is an excellent demonstration of these considerations. Rather than condemning or belittling his daughter's interest in biting her nails Erickson takes her desire seriously, thereby establishing rapport. He then engages her in a behavior that seems completely reasonable given her situation, but it is nevertheless a behavior that Erickson is confident will soon trans-form nailbiting into a distasteful chore.

At first glance Erickson's instructions to the balding woman and his

daughter may seem to be straightforward examples of brief therapy's "prescribing the symptom" intervention. It is not, and nowhere in our transcripts of Erickson's work do we find an example of his merely prescribing the symptom. As an intervention,
symptom prescription takes advantage of the innate contrariness
of some individuals. By telling a client to go ahead with, or
even increase, his compulsive behavior the therapist robs the
client of the unconscious and somehow satisfying pleasure of doing
something that is normally and otherwise condemnable. This
leaves discontinuing the behavior as the only means the client
has left to assert his or her independence of the desires of
others.

> The most important Achilles heel of these interven-
> tions, however, is the necessity of successfully moti-
> vating somebody to carry out our instructions . . .
> Thus, one potential source of failure is the inability
> to present the intervention in a "language" which
> makes sense to our client and which therefore makes
> him willing to accept and carry out the instructions.
> (from *Change*, Watzlawick, Weakland, and Fisch.
> p. 115).

If you were to prescribe the symptom for the hair-pulling woman,
for example, you would tell her that she is to pull her hair out three
times as often. The onus of having to engage in such behavior could
indeed compel her to discontinue it, provided first that you actually
could get her to pull her hair out three times as often. Erickson does
not tell this woman to pull her hair out more often. Instead, he
attaches to it an additional piece of behavior, the burden of which the
client is unable to separate from her initial hair-pulling behavior. By
leaving the woman's hair-pulling behavior intact, Erickson avoids an
almost certain confrontation. The fact, particulars, and ramifications
of her behavior have undoubtedly been central to much of her personal and social experience in the past, and so the context of hair-
pulling is a highly loaded one. After years of introspection and consultation with others the justifications for her hair-pulling behavior will
be readily available. Erickson avoids this historical mire by skirting it,
rather than trying to change or slog through it. What is important is
that one get the client to the other side, where the naturally occurring

environment of feed forward and feedback generated by the new behaviors and generalizations can take over the task of solidifying and perpetuating those new behaviors.

Reproduction of this pattern is straightforward in terms of its structure. Simply accept the client's unwanted behavior, then attach as a contingent to it some additional piece of behavior that will eventually prove decisively burdensome. The trick, as stated above, is to devise an additional behavior that HAS such a compelling effect, to be able to exert the influence necessary to engage your client in the behavior, and to be able to create for your client the contingent relationship between the compulsive and assigned behaviors. Generating compellingly burdensome behaviors will be dependent upon your experience in utilizing them (that is, you learn by using the pattern). The influence necessary to create the contingent relationship and to get clients to engage in the assigned behavior will, for the most part, depend upon your ability to secure and maintain rapport (as described above, primarily through acceptance of the unwanted behavior, pacing of their ongoing experience, and pacing of their model of the world when selecting the burdensome behavior.) The following examples illustrate the pattern clearly:

> I had one doctor who told me, "I go to bed about 11:00 and I don't go to sleep 'til 5 or 5:30 and I have to be in my office at 7:00. All through college and medical school I *promised* myself that I would read Dickens, Thackery and Dostoevski, Voltaire, and Scott. And I was working too hard to get through medical school and then I got married and got to working too hard in order to support my family. I've got six children. And I've never *done* that reading and I suffer from insomnia. After work and supporting the family, no sleep and I'm just plain miserable."
> I said, "Doctor, if you want to get over your insomnia I know a sure way of doing it. Do you have a mantle piece in your home?" He said, "I have a fireplace with a mantle piece." I said, "Fix up a light on your mantle piece, get a set of Dickens. If you are going to stay awake from 11 to 5, stay awake standing at the mantle piece reading

Dickens." By the time he got through the first volume he said, "Please, can I sit down to read?" I said, "Yes" . . . then he came to me and said, "I fall asleep in the chair." I said, "All right, get a clock with an illuminated dial. Go to bed at your usual time and fifteen minutes after you go to bed, if you can read the time on that clock, get up and read Dickens standing at the mantle piece." He learned to sleep. He also found time to read Dickens, Voltaire, Scott and Dostoevski.

There was a man who had a bachelor son. He and his son ran a real estate office. And when the man's wife died, he developed insomnia. And he rolled and tossed . . . by the time he got to sleep it was time to get up. He came and told me this. I said, "Where are you living now?" "My bachelor son and I live together." "Who does the housework?" "We share that . . . we share most of it, but I can't *stand* waxing the floor so my son always does that." I said, "I have a remedy for your insomnia. You won't like it but it WILL be effective. Very shortly it will cause you to lose some hours of sleep, but not many. Instead of going to bed tonight take a can of Johnson's floor wax and YOU polish that hardwood floor all night long. Go to the office the next day, do your work there, return home. Eat your meal and at bedtime get out the wax and polish the floor all night long. You won't lose much sleep . . . just two nights. Meanwhile you're getting cured of your insomnia. I think it will be only two nights." I think on the third night he decided to rest his eyes and he awoke 7:00 the next morning. He came and told me. I said, "All right, you have a clock with an illuminated dial in full view on your dresser and the can of floor wax beside the clock with a polishing rag. If you can read the time in fifteen minutes after you go to bed, you're in for a night of polishing the floor." He told me later, "I sleep *regularly.*" Why bother doing some plain psychotherapy

on the man? I created a situation and he'd do ANYTHING
to sleep and get out of doing it!

In both of the cases cited above Erickson engages the insomniacs
in behavior that they are certain to eventually want to renounce—
standing and reading at the mantlepiece for the first, polishing floors
for the second. And in both cases the lesson is so thoroughly learned
that the mere threat of repeating the learning experience is sufficient
to send them to dream land within 15-minutes. As far as the selection
of prescribed behavior, the first case described is an example of selecting an experience that anyone is likely to find profoundly tedious—
standing all night. The second example is one of selecting a burdensome adjunctive behavior unique to that client—polishing floors. Be-
sides being unpleasant things to do, both standing and scrubbing floors
are inherently tiring tasks, and so will make the prospect of a comfortable bed that much more attractive. Erickson creates in these insomniacs sincere motivation to learn new sleep behavior by making the
avoidance of these tedious tasks contingent upon developing the ability to go to sleep quickly. That they actually followed his instructions
and accepted them as contingencies . . .

One of my daughters once asked me, "Daddy, why do
people DO the crazy things you tell them to do?" I said,
"Because they know I mean it."

Footnotes

1. For one of the best examples of calibration to patterned sequences of behavior see the
opening interchange between that master of deduction, Sherlock Holmes and his chroni-
cler, Watson, in *The Cardboard Box.*

CHAPTER 6

Snake Dance

Annotated Transcript

O ne of the accomplishments for which the Hopi Indians are famous is a ceremony in which various members of the tribe dance
while holding in their mouths live rattlesnakes. Now how does one go
about *practicing* such a dance? You could start out by learning the
chants and their music. Then the dance steps. You could practice
those steps with a stick in your mouth. And learning how to properly
address rattlesnakes might also be highly recommended. You could
practice all of these skills endlessly. But at some point you have to pick
up a live rattlesnake, place it in your mouth . . . and dance.

Throughout the previous chapters we have endeavored to impress
you with the fact that Erickson's work was not the product of any one
of the patterns described here (or elsewhere, for that matter), but a
product of the *simultaneous* utilization of many, if not all, of those
patterns. Even though a particular case history was selected because
of the clarity with which it pointed-up the particular pattern we
wished to describe, we also tried to mention Erickson's use of other,
previously described patterns within that same case study. Certainly,
every example of Erickson's therapeutic work with which we are
familiar involves the establishing of rapport, some altering or utilization of reference frames, and the instigation of some behavior. These

three attributes of his approach are, as we said in Chapter II, a function of how Erickson is organized as an individual, and so are characteristic of virtually everything he does. In this volume we have fractionated this larger structure of therapy organization into "smaller" patterns descriptive of his behavior within that structure, and, in so doing, have run the risk of conferring upon those patterns the status or aura of "techniques." It is true that they can be used as techniques, but the person who does so runs the risk of responding to techniques, rather than to *people*, of trying to make clients conform to your techniques, rather than tailoring your communications and interventions to the *client's* peculiarities. It should be remembered that most of what we have described in this book as being patterns of Erickson's work are our inventions, and are not at all necessarily a codified part of *Erickson's* understanding of Erickson. These patterns are model descriptions of his *behavior,* which is a natural and inevitable function of how he is organized as an individual. Therefore, these patterns are not necessarily techniques that he knowingly applies, but are patterns within his ongoing behavior, available for use when appropriate, when called for, just as the syntax you use to formulate well-formed sentences is a part of your behavior, operating not as a piece of technology intentionally applied, but unconsciously as needed and, so, gracefully and congruently. It is the fact that these patterns do operate "automatically" that makes it possible for Erickson to utilize them simultaneously—the ability of your analogue and word structure to convey many levels of communication far exceeds your conscious mind's ability to compute and monitor those levels. For anyone interested in reproducing the kind of therapeutic successes that characterized Erickson's work, then, your goal should be to incorporate the patterns described in this volume (and in the others listed in the bibliography) into your ongoing (ie. unconscious) behavior.

In order to assuage some of the onus of "technique" inherent in the piecemeal presentation of the patterns so far, and to provide you with a more extensive reference experience for the integrated utilization of those patterns, we now present an annotated transcript of Erickson describing a case that involved more extended treatment than most of those previously cited in this book, and which illustrates his utilization of most of the therapeutic patterns described in this book.

I got a phone call one February, a woman's voice said, I'm an M.D., my husband is an M.D. and our fourteen year old daughter is suffering from Anorexia nervosa. During the last month in the hospital she has lost five pounds and she's down to 61 pounds and it's obvious she is going to die. I've read *Uncommon Therapy,* so has my husband, and we think if our daughter can be helped you can do it. Will you take her as a patient?" I said, "Give me a couple of days to think it over and call me." She called me a couple days later and I agreed to see the daughter. Lori and her mother arrived in February. Lori was a very bright girl, fourteen years old, sixty-one pounds. And, in Anorexia nervosa there is a peculiar emotional relationship with the parents. And there is a peculiar religiosity about the condition—they are sin free, they are meek and mild, they will do no wrong, and they see nothing wrong with eating an oyster cracker and a glass of water for a day's food intake . . . And they are SO subservient, *ever* so good, so sweet. You can't anger them at *all*.

So when Lori and her mother came in I looked at that emaciated girl and sent her out of the room and told the mother, "I've seen about fifty Anorexia nervosa patients in hospital situations and they *all died.* And in the hospital they are treated professionally, with dignity . . . properly, with the doctor's self-respect maintained carefully.

In his description of Lori, Erickson is identifying several important aspects of her model of the world, all of which can be condensed into the generalization that she is "sin free". Therefore, doing what is right and proper is of fundamental importance to her. As you read through this transcript notice that Erickson consistently matches and utilizes this important personal criterion of Lori's by being himself concerned about what is or is not "proper" (content rapport). In fact, even when Erickson subsequently challenges Lori's generalizations about her ubiquitous goodness he does so within the framework of what is "right and proper" (we want to emphasize here that having rapport with a client does *not* mean that the client "likes" you, but that your client has the experience of communicating with someone who understands his or her model of the world).

With his statement to Lori's mother about the fatal consequences of Anorexia nervosa Erickson does two things: First, he establishes rapport by matching mother's own worst fears about Lori dying, rather than, for example, reassuring her that Lori will be fine (which might have indicated to Lori's mother that Erickson does not fully appreciate the gravity of the situation.) Second, by implying almost no hope Erickson increases the mother's potential for response to any subsequent corrective possibilities he might offer her. By following his statement about Anorexics dying with the statement about the "professional dignity" of hospital treatment Erickson builds a new generalization in mother regarding the ineffectuality of normal and dignified treatment approaches. This insures that mother will not interfere with Erickson's treatment should it become "unprofessional".

Now I want you to sign an agreement that I've explained to you fully about Anorexia nervosa, and the hazard to life that it is for your daughter. And then I want you to sign another agreement that in no way will you hold ME responsible in case your daughter dies. And you will let me do whatever I wish with your daughter." The mother signed the papers. Of course, signing them had a psychological effect on the mother. They had no legal standing at all.

Understanding that he is going to need mother's compliance, Erickson goes on to reinforce in her behavior the generalization he had created, just before, regarding her acceptance of unorthodox treatment. Note also that the intonation pattern that Erickson uses in defining the agreement regarding "responsibility" ("in no way will you hold ME responsible . . .") implies the question, "Who, then, *is* responsible?", and the likelihood that mother's answer is that she is herself responsible.

And then I started an interview with Lori. "What grade are you in at school?" Mother answered. "When is your birthday?" Mother answered. I let that go on for three days. And every night of those three days Lori whimpered . . . kept her mother awake. Lori whimpered softly and gently . . . nonetheless, her mother heard it. So on the fourth interview I asked Lori a question . . . mother answered, I said, "Mother, I asked that question to *Lori!* Henceforth would you PLEASE KEEP YOUR MOUTH SHUT!! If I ask Lori a question I want *Lori* to answer it." She flushed and closed her trap. Of course telling her mother to keep her trap shut altered the emotional relationship be-

Several times in describing this case Erickson mentions the "peculiar relationship" between Lori and her mother without further specification, and, so, we do not always know how his interventions relate to that relationship. In this section we do know, however, that Erickson identifies a pattern of behavior involving Lori keeping mom from sleeping, and mom keeping Lori from answering questions, a pattern which he disrupts by telling mom to shut up. Note, however, that before rebuking Lori's mother, Erickson allows them to clearly establish their patterns of behavior so that his accusation and condemnation of mother's behavior is undeniably accurate and not dismissable as a transient

tween Lori and her mother. She and her mother had a peculiar emotional relationship.

piece of behavior. Erickson not only alters their pattern of interacting behaviors, he also gives Lori the opportunity to include in her model of the world the possibility that her mother can act improperly and be the *justifiable* recipient of anger and censure.

And then I asked Lori about her whimpering at night and she said she didn't MEAN to keep her mother awake. I said, "Well Lori, when anybody whimpers and keeps another person awake they are *offending* against that person. And people who offend *knowingly* against another person should be punished." And Lori meekly agreed.

This is an excellent example of Erickson using Lori's own model of the world to alter her perspective. As one who is "sin free" and "ever so good", Lori must certainly agree that it is offensive to disturb her mother's sleep. The next statement about the appropriateness of punishing knowing "offenders" is offered as an accepted and general rule of conduct, with which Lori agrees, but by that acceptance she not only agrees that it is proper that she be punished, but inherits the implication that she did it *knowingly* as well. In this way, then, Erickson begins to replace Lori's "ever so good" generalizations about herself with generalizations which admit of a much wider range of behavior and experience.

I said, "I won't punish you . . . you didn't offend against ME. You offended against your mother. I'm going to instruct your mother to punish you properly and reasonably.

We want to draw your attention to Erickson's decision to punish Lori *properly*, utilizing the importance Lori places on "doing right"—rather than merely punishing her he punished her *properly*. (Also, in the segment immediately above he establishes that it is "proper" that she be punished.)

I sent the girl into the other room and told mother, "Any food is punishment for Lori so feed her a scrambled egg. Her stomach won't know the difference between punishment and food." Her mother eagerly scrambled two eggs and fed them to her. And Lori

Erickson utilizes Lori's distaste for eating and the necessity of her being punished to create a way of getting her to eat that is reasonable and acceptable, given her criteria of doing whatever is proper.

meekly took her punishment—not food, but punishment . . . her stomach started a new psychological routine.

In the first three days I told Lori, "Your mother brought you here for me to improve your eating habits. What you eat is *your* business, none of mine. I'm a doctor and I'm only entitled to look after your health and you seem to be in good health, but you may be neglecting some things. Now whether you EAT or not is none of MY business, but as a doctor it IS my business to know that you brush your teeth three times a day. And, you ought to use a mouth wash to loosen the detritus in your mouth and to wash it out and you're not to swallow the toothpaste OR the mouth wash. Now do you *agree* to THAT?" And Lori meekly agreed as I expected she probably would. And with that religiosity, and a solemn promise made, Lori was caught. I told her she could use any fluoride toothpaste she wished . . . as for the mouth wash I thought an EXCELLENT one would be raw cod liver oil. Do you know the usual pattern of a mouth washed with raw cod liver oil? She would want to eat the dirt from the garden . . . ANYTHING to get rid of that taste.

Here Erickson establishes cultural rapport by telling Lori that he is not going to do what her parents want him to do and that that matter is her personal business—two perceptions which are almost certainly of importance to a teenager. Erickson then claims his proper purview of authority to be her health, and asks the ambiguous question, "Now do you *agree* to THAT?" "That" is deliberately unspecified so that it would be ambiguous to Lori whether or not her disagreement would include the question of Erickson's lack of authority over her eating. Having been confirmed in his proper authority over her oral hygiene, Erickson was free to direct her in a behavior the *natural consequences* of which would be to WANT to eat something (to refuse to use the cod liver oil would be to offend Dr. Erickson and go back on her word) an example of the pattern discussed in "Sow's Ears" in Chapter V.

And the therapy with Lori was to tell her stories, anecdotes . . . slightly risque stories. I told her how my mother had been born in a super deluxe log cabin in Wisconsin. Super deluxe because it had a wooden floor, a trap door in the floor, and a vegetable bin underneath the floor. THAT made it super deluxe. I explained that the log

Although the stories originally told to Lori by Erickson were undoubtedly gold mines of hypnosis, metaphor, and therapeutic patterns, even this brief description is richly veined, and worth your careful attention. Erickson elicits in Lori the experience of being "interested", then uses the ambiguity of "miner"-*minor* (i.e. Lori) and the metaphor of cabin I was born in had three sides made of logs, one side was a mountain side and it had a dirt floor up in the Sierra Nevada mountains. And of course to meet someone whose mother was born in a log cabin who was also born in a log cabin would be of interest to a bright child. And there was nothing Lori could do to prevent her from being interested. And I told her how my mother ran a boarding house for a mining camp. I explained how the freight train came to the miner's camp only twice a year which meant you ordered your flour, salt, pepper, baking powder, sugar everything six months in advance. The trick of the job is to *figure how much you need* of all those things. I told Lori how my mother felt sorry for the miners because they got sick and tired of dried apple pie, dried peach pie, dried apricot pie, dried prune pie, dried raisin pie . . . and she felt so sorry for them that she INVENTED a pie for them. She made a custard out of cornstarch and dumped in enough cinnamon to make it dark brown . . . all the miners liked it, and it's my favorite pie too! Now Lori's family traveled all over the world. They were great travelers. And they're wealthy. They stay at the best places and eat the best food. And here was a cinnamon pie . . . something she had never HEARD of.

And I told her *boring* stories, *IRRITAT-ING* stories. Dr. Pearson of Michigan sat in on one of our sessions. At the end of it he wiped his brow and said, "You ran that poor girl up and down the gamut of emotion over and over

ordering provisions as a way of making a post hypnotic suggestion about ordering her life for the next six months with respect to food. Erickson then goes on to a direct imbedded command to "figure out how much you (Lori) need of all those things (food)". He then takes the miner/minor through the experience of *wanting something new* to eat, being curious about food, and getting something new and satisfying to eat. (The reader is encouraged to refer to *Patterns of the Hypnotic Techniques of Milton H. Erickson, M.D.*, by Bandler and Grinder, and to *Therapeutic Metaphors* by David Gordon, for a thorough presentation of the patterns of hypnosis and metaphor which can be found in this description)

Much of Erickson's work with Lori is directed towards broadening her range of internal responses and external behaviors. Her response in almost every situation has been meek piety, which is certainly inappropriate in *all* situations.

again. I had a hard time TAKING it."
But Lori took it. During the first two
weeks Lori gained three pounds, lost
one and gained it back in two weeks
time.

Erickson uses his stories to access in Lori
the whole range of human experience.
This provides her with the opportunity
to alter her perspective about the pious
purity and constancy of her internal experiences, and with the opportunity to
learn and/or relearn those experiential
possibilities she needs in order to respond generatively (sorting for rele-
vance).

And one day I told Lori, "You're a
coward. You're a liar. I can prove it."
Lori meekly protested. I said, "Oh yes
you ARE a coward and you're a *liar*. I
can prove it. Hit me on the arm." Now
Lori, she was angry within but control-
ling her anger, concealing it. Finally
she reached over and tapped me. I
said, "That's right Lori, now you've
proved it. You merely tapped my arm
and that is a non-verbal *lie* because
you're implying that a tap is a hit. And
you're too much of a coward to RE-
ALLY hit my arm." Lori's face con-
torted and she poked my arm and
dashed out of the room and closed the
door behind her. She came back in a
few moments later dried eyed, dried
faced, and sat down meekly. I said,
"Lori, I ALREADY knew you were a
liar and a coward . . . you didn't need
to prove it twice! Now you did hit me
but you *ran away*. And in running
away you had two purposes—to es-
cape any retaliation on my part, so
you're a coward, and you ran away so
I wouldn't see the *tears* in your eyes
and you came back dried eyed, dried
faced, and you're pretending you
didn't *shed tears,* and that's a lie. You
did." Lori looked troubled.

Once again Erickson challenges Lori's
meekness by accessing in her anger, frustration, embarassment, and so on. As described above, Erickson has been using
stories to get Lori to access in her internal experience these kinds of emotions
and responses. In calling Lori a coward
and a liar, and getting her to hit him,
Erickson is not only accessing those internal experiences but he is now forcing
her to demonstrate them in her behavior
(her faces, running away, crying, drying
her eyes.)

A few hours later I said, "Mother, stand up! How tall are you?" "5 feet 6." (Actually I think Mother lied. Mrs. Erickson and I both felt she was about 5 feet 9.) "How much do you weigh?" "One hundred and eighteen pounds . . . same weight I was when I got married." So I went into a state of emotional shock: "You, a forty year old woman, and the mother of five children, weighing one hundred and eighteen pounds, 5 feet 6?! And YOU HAVE THE GALL TO BRING YOUR DAUGHTER TO ME BECAUSE YOU THOUGHT *SHE* WAS UNDER-NOURISHED? What about yourself?! Aren't you ashamed of yourself?! Admit it!" And, of course, Lori got a new emotional look at her mother. And I turned to Lori and said, "Lori, your mother is underweight and she needs to eat better. I want you to see to it that she does clean up her plate at *every meal*. And if she DOESN'T do it *properly* I want you to tell me the very next day."

Note that Lori's mother describes herself as being three inches shorter than she actually was, and that she is also concerned about not gaining weight (as is indicated by her comparisons between her present weight and that as a bride). Erickson takes a highly valued criterion of mother's regarding the importance of protecting the health of her daughter and attaches it to mother's own weight-watching behavior, thereby building in her the generalization that her behavior affects her daughter's behavior (sorting for BIG liabilities). By pointing out to mother that she is also shamefully under-weight and assigning Lori the task of looking after her mother's diet, Erickson reverses their relationship and esta-blishes equivalence between their prob-lems. It is no longer that Lori is anorexic, but that "it is not good to be under-weight" and both mother and Lori "hap-pen" to be underweight. In this way Erickson alters their perspective of Lori's situation from being endemic and perhaps enduringly characteristic to being common and transient. This change in perspective is important both for immediate remediation (in terms of the immediate goal of reversing the trend) and in terms of Lori's subsequent functioning at home as well, for it makes it possible for Lori and her mother to respond to future fluctuations in Lori's weight as being a question of *appropriate* weight, rather than being indicative of a possible return to "anorexia nervosa". By having Lori supervise her mother's eat-ing habits Erickson is also having Lori install in her own behavioral repetoire the very distinctions and reference ex-periences she will later need in order to assess and supervise her own diet.

So one day Lori came in and said, "I forgot to tell you yesterday, that the other day Mother saved half of her hamburger, wrapped it up in a napkin and kept it for a midnight snack." So I developed another emotional shock. "I thought you were suppose to clean up your plate? You can *buy* a midnight snack if you wish, and you don't cheat on your luncheon. Now you've offended against me and so I'm going to punish you. And Lori, you were supposed to report your mother's misbehavior the very next day. You've delayed a whole day. So you've offended against me and YOU'RE going to be punished for offending against me. Now Mother, tomorrow you bring some bread and cheese into my kitchen in the main house and I'll have to make you a cheese sandwich, Erickson style." (You put a layer of cheese on a slice of bread, put it under the broiler, melt it, bring it out, turn it over, put another layer of cheese, put it under the broiler, melt it, bring it out and *eat* it.) "Lori, your mother is going to eat a cheese sandwich Erickson style and so are you." They showed up the next day with the bread and cheese. They made the sandwiches under my eagle eye and they ate them. Of course, Lori's physiology took care of that matter. Now Lori and her mother were great travelers. They would take off days to go to various parts of Arizona. I asked if she could take Lori to the Grand Canyon. She said, "Yes". I said, "Now Mother, Lori must be reminded to take her mouth wash with her. And Lori, I want you to promise to take your mouth wash WITH you." Now any reasonably in-

Erickson arranges for Lori two opportunities to break promises and, so, presents her with uncontestable evidence that she is not wholly virtuous, but has instead other (even if distasteful) dimensions to her personality. Erickson utilizes the necessity of "punishing" Lori and her mother as an opportunity to challenge their rigid notions about food (orienting them towards flexibility).

telligent child who has raw cod liver oil as a mouth wash, going to the Grand Canyon, is naturally going to forget and leave it behind! I told her mother, "Once you've reminded her to take it with her, never again do you mention mouth wash to her, neither will I, and you will never notice that the bottle is missing." So I put a burden of GUILT on Lori and it didn't agree with her identification with Christ. She WAS guilty. She had PURPOSELY left that bottle behind her, as I knew she would.

And I raised the question, "Now Lori, I don't think you enjoy being my patient. I know I wouldn't enjoy being someone's patient who could treat me the way I've treated YOU." And now, "Are you enjoying visiting Arizona here and there? I know you don't want to stay here and be my patient forever, nor do I WANT you to be my patient forever. I think you should be thinking about how much you should weigh in order to go home. Now I might want you to weigh 85 pounds. You might prefer to weigh 75 pounds. We might compromise on 80 pounds. And Mother, I think you ought to weigh 130 pounds. You may decide on 125 pounds. But bear in mind the daily variance of weight is about a pound and a half. Now you choose your weight. And when you reach those weights you can go home." And Lori chose 75, which meant 76½. The mother chose 125, which meant 126½. And then I lowered the boom on Lori again. I said, "Now, when you weigh that 76½ pounds, you can go back home. And if you don't gain 5 *pounds* in that

Rather than raising as a question whether or not Lori will gain weight, Erickson presupposes that Lori will be gaining weight and that the only question is, "how much?" He is reorienting her, then, towards the future. Erickson then describes the range of weight which could satisfy the question of "how much", and, in so doing, he establishes what he considers to be a lower limit while Lori and her mother enjoy the illusion of choice. By making Lori's return to Phoenix dependent upon Lori's ability to match a criterion set by Erickson rather than being contingent upon her mother's personal responses, Erickson negates the usefulness of Lori's renewing her previous behavior with respect to her mother since her ability to affect her mother through abstinence will not influence whether or not Lori returns (abstinence will, in fact, result in returning to the tortures of Phoenix—Sow's Ears).

first month that you are home your mother is under MY orders to bring you back here.''

The mother had kept in contact with Lori's father and he flew down with her brother and sister. I interviewed him separately. "How tall, how old, your weight? So you're five pounds underweight . . . why?" He said, "For preventive measures against diabetes." "Any history of diabetes in the family?" He said, "No, it's just a preventive measure." I said, "In other words, you have *gambled* being five pounds underweight *against your daughter's life!!* What do you think about yourself, gambling in that fashion? Are you ashamed?" He was *properly* humiliated. I sent him out and had the two older siblings come in. I asked them, "When did Lori first start developing her sickness?" They said, "About a year ago." "When you offered her an apple or candy or cookies what happened?" "She always said, 'Keep it for yourself, I don't deserve it' ", they said. So then I read them the riot act about their *willful* robbing of their sister of her constitutional rights to receive gifts. I rebuked them thoroughly. And they were feeling very apologetic for depriving their sister of her constitutional rights. I sent them out and called Lori in. I said, "Lori, in the past your brother and sister and parents have often offered you things to eat—candy, fruit—you always refuse them. Are you aware that you are depriving them of their constitutional rights to GIVE you things?! Now aren't you ashamed of yourself?" And Lori meekly agreed.

Here Erickson uses the pattern of sorting for BIG liabilities as a way of systematically altering the perspective of Lori and her family in a way that insures that their future responses to one another are supportive of Lori's needs. Like Lori's mother, her father is inappropriately concerned about his weight. By connecting father's inappropriate concern about his own weight (i.e., there is no history of diabetes) to Lori's behavior Erickson offers Lori's father a new perspective which involves the recognition that his behavior has an important impact on Lori's behavior, necessitating father's abandonment of the importance of being underweight in favor of being of *appropriate* weight. Erickson then goes on to use the same pattern with Lori and her siblings to insure that in the future any offers of food are pressed by her brother and sister and accepted by Lori. Instead of accepting Lori's declinings of food they will, in their behavior, become more insistent that she accept the food in an effort to preserve her "constitutional rights to receive gifts".

Now Lori and her mother attended my daughter Roxanna's wedding. And I was careful not to observe her but my daughters have sharp eyes and they reported that Lori ate some wedding cake. At the time of their departure Lori asked her mother to take a polaroid picture of her sitting on my lap in the wheel chair. When Lori got home she found a letter awaiting her. It read "What you weigh is nobody's business except yours and your conscience's. Your weight lies between you and your conscience. You don't have to report your weight." She sent me her school picture in September and it showed a reasonably well-nourished girl. Christmas they went to the Bahamas and Lori sent me her Christmas picture . . . Hard to believe it was the same girl . . . from knobby knees to slick chick.

Now Lori has continued correspondence with me. She writes very beautiful letters. Her family traveled over to Europe one summer and Lori kept a catalog of the trip . . . it was all about the international foods. There was ALWAYS an indirect mention of food. When I told Lori that I asked the International Society to make note of my 75th birthday by planting a tree, she wrote back, "I'll plant a plum tree for you." All together I spent twenty hours with that girl. You just meet a patient's emotional needs and don't be afraid to tell a mother to keep her trap shut and *mean* it . . . that reconstructed the mother daughter relationship.

Lori's eating of the wedding cake was an indication that she was learning to eat appropriately (that is, in relation to the context she was in and her own needs) rather than in relation to a rigid concept *about* the appropriateness of eating itself. With this (and probably other demonstrations not mentioned) Erickson, in his letter to her, turns over to Lori the responsibility for monitoring her own behavior tying her weight to her conscience).

CHAPTER 7

Origin of the Specie

As we have said all along and in various ways, Milton Erickson is a man whose therapeutic wizardry is a function of his model of the world, rather than the application of codified techniques. That what Erickson does therapeutically is an inevitable behavioral expression of his model of the world does not mean, however, that his behavior is beyond characterization and modeling. It is not. While no one pretends to be able to reproduce the content of Erickson's experience, the patterns of behavior with which Erickson *organized* that content can be modeled and passed on to others. What shaped those patterns, that model? He did not sit down one day and decide just how he should think about people and changing them, but like us all was shaped by his experiences, in the same way that he created experiences for his clients. Nowhere is it more evident than in Erickson's own descriptions of his personal experiences that what he learned he learned in those little everyday events that no one notices yet everyone lives, and that what he taught his clients was just what he himself had learned . . . and he taught those things to others the way he learned them, through the little everyday things that no one notices yet everyone lives.

When I first went to college, I got interested in memories. I thought it over carefully: how soon would there be enough learning by an infant to permit memories? And what kind of memories would they be? Now I recall my first spanking at the age of nine months. And I wrote it out in detail and when I went back to the farm, I asked my parents if there had been another cabin in the Sierra Nevada Mountains. They said, "Yes, the cabin we use to live in was way down the valley . . . several miles away there was another cabin." I said, "Had you ever visited the Camerons when I was an infant?" Mother and Father thought it over and they finally recalled that they had made a visit there. And I said, "You wore long dresses then and you sat on a chair and I saw Mrs. Cameron pick up something and put it somewhere and it made a beautiful splash of color. So I crept over, took something and put it there and made a beautiful splash of color and Mrs. Cameron, only I didn't know her name, spanked me. I was enraged. I crept up to my mother's chair and hid behind her skirts." My mother and father recalled, "Oh yes, you threw something in the fireplace at the Cameron cabin and Mrs. Cameron picked you up and spanked you and explained, 'When a child is wrong, you spank him right away.' " I still feel that horrible sense of outrage— why could she put something there?—I get spanked for it! It was just plain outrageous!!

My next memory was there were two objects triangular in shape. I subsequently realized that they were women. And they were showing me a Christmas tree with a lighted candle on it. And in the background there was a two legged thing with a lot of hair on its face. I asked my parents if there had been a Christmas tree? They agreed, "Yes there had been," but they couldn't remember that particular Christmas and the question came down to dating that memory. And that memory was finally identified as December 25th, 1902. I was one year and three weeks old. And my parents dated that memory because that hairy-faced man was my father trying on an outfit for my mother and sister. And my parents dated it by working out when my father shaved off his beard. And in February 1903 my father told my mother, "I'm tired of the boy grabbing my whiskers to pull himself up." So they clearly identified the memory. Those two peculiar triangular objects and that two legged creature with a lot of hair on its face . . . when you give yourself permission to remember things it is astonishing because we all have the attitude, "Oh that was kid stuff". Kid stuff is very important, it is the background for knowing things.

I was returning from high school one day and a runaway horse with his bridle on sped past a group of us into a farmer's yard, looking for a drink of water. He was perspiring heavily. And the farmer didn't recognize it so we cornered it. I hopped on the horse's back . . . since he had a bridle on I managed to take hold of the tick rein and said "Giddy-up" . . . headed for the highway. I knew the horse would turn in the right direction . . . I didn't know what the right direction was. And the horse trotted and galloped along. Now and then he would forget he was on the highway and start into a field. So I would pull on him a bit and call his attention to the fact the highway was where he was supposed to be. And finally, about four miles from where I boarded him, he turned into a farm yard and the farmer said, "So that's how that critter came back! Where did you find him?" I said, "About four miles from here." "How did you know you should come here?" I said, "I didn't know, the horse knew . . . all I did was keep his attention on the road." I think that's the way you do psychotherapy.

Now I'm going to speak to another situation, the thing

that influenced me most in shaping my thinking in the matter of psychotherapy. I was living on a farm in Wisconsin in an area where an eighth grade graduation was the ultimate in education. High school was not approved of. Any boy or girl that went to high school, they were on their way to be educated fools. And that was not approved of. When I was about ten years old my father sent me to the neighboring village about a mile away on an errand. And, of course, as I came into the village, my schoolmates this one summer came rushing to meet me and they told me the exciting news—'Joe is back!' I had never heard of Joe, but they soon informed me of who Joe was. Joe, at the age of twelve, a farmer's son and only child, had been expelled from school because of brutality and beating up the other children, his vandalism, his incorrigible behavior . . . and he had stabbed his father's hogs, and calves and cows and horses with pitch forks. And he several times tried to set the barn to fire and the house afire. Well, at the age of twelve his parents took him to court, had him committed to the Industrial School for boys. At the age of fifteen the Industrial School paroled him. On the way home Joe committed some burglaries and was picked up by the police and promptly returned to the Industrial School, where he had to stay until he was twenty-one years old. By that time his parents were dead and they disposed of their property leaving Joe without any inheritance. And when he was discharged at age twenty-one he was given a suit and $10, and he headed for Milwaukee . . . was shortly arrested for burglary and sent to the Young Men's Reformatory in Green Bay. He served every day of that sentence—in other words, no time off for good behavior. He was released from the reformatory, he went into the town of Green Bay, and committed some more burglaries. The police picked him up and he was sent to state prison. And when he completed every day of that sentence he was released, went into the village and committed some more burglaries and was arrested by another policeman and given a second term in the state prison. After serving every day of that term, he returned to the village. That day I arrived in the village it was his fourth day in town. Each of the three previous days he had spent standing beside the cash register estimating the day's take of the merchants at three different stores. And all of them knew that Joe had broken into their store and stolen a lot of things. A man who owned a motor boat had found his motor boat was missing. And the morning I arrived Joe was sitting on a bench under the store awning staring into the distance. Now it happened that there was a farmer about three miles from the village. A farmer who had three hundred acres of company land. He was a very rich man, had beautiful buildings, and to work three hundred acres it requires a hired man. And his daughter Susie had graduated from eighth grade, she was about five feet ten, and she could work alongside any man in the community. She could pitch hay, plow fields, help with the butchering . . . any task she could handle. The entire community felt bad about Susie. She was a good looking girl, she was famous for her housekeeping, her dressmaking and for her cooking, and she was an old maid at twenty-three years. And that should not be. Everybody thought Susie was too choosy. On that particular day when I went to the village on the errand, Susie's father's hired hand quit because of a death in the family and said he would not be back. And Susie's father sent her into the village on an errand. Susie arrived, tied up the horse and buggy, came walking down the street. And Joe stood up and blocked her pathway. And Joe looked her up and down very thoroughly, quietly . . . and Susie with equal poise looked him up and down very thoroughly. Finally

Joe said, "Can I take you to the dance next Friday?" Now the village always had a weekly dance on Friday nights for all the young people. And Susie was very much in demand at those dances and she regularly drove in and attended the dance. And when Joe said, "Can I take you to the dance next Friday?" Susie said coolly, "You can if you're a gentleman." Joe stepped out of her way. She performed her errand, went back. And the next morning the merchants were very glad to find boxes full of stolen goods at their front doors. And the motor boat had returned. And Joe was seen walking down the highway towards Susie's father's farm. Word soon got around that he had asked Susie's father for the job of hired hand, and he was hired. And made a magnificent wage of $15 per month. He was allowed to have his meals in the kitchen with the family. And Susie's father said, "We'll fix a room for you in the barn." In Wisconsin when the temperatures are down to 35° below zero you really need a well insulated room in the barn. Joe turned out to be the best hired hand that community had ever seen. Joe worked from sun up to long past sun down, seven days a week. Joe was six feet three, a very able bodied man and, of course, Joe always walked to the village on Friday nights to attend the dance. Susie drove in to attend the dance. And much to the ire of the other young men Susie usually danced with Joe every dance. And Joe's size made them wary of pointing out to Joe the error of his way by appropriating Susie. In just about a year the community was buzzing with gossip because Susie and Joe were seen going out Saturday evening for a drive, or 'sparking', as the term was used. And there was even more gossip the next day—on Sunday—Susie and Joe went to church together. And there after for some months Joe and Susie went for a drive every Saturday evening and to church on Sunday. And after some months of this Susie and Joe were married. And Joe moved from the barn into the house. He was still the best hired man imaginable and Joe and his father-in-law, with some aid of Susie, ran the farm. And Joe was such a good worker that when a neighbor got sick, Joe was the first one to show up to help with the chores. And they soon forgot all about Joe's history of being an ex-convict.

Now when I decided to go to high school a lot of the neighbors were displeased. But Joe encouraged me to go to high school and encouraged a lot of other kids to go to high school. I decided to go to the University—the neighbors groaned about that Erickson kid becoming an educated fool and Joe encouraged me to go to college. He thought it was a very excellent idea for all young people to go to college. And Joe's popularity in the neighborhood was such that he was elected to the school board. And at the first meeting of the school board all the parents were there. And Joe opened the meeting by saying, "You folks have elected me president of the school board. You gave me the most votes and that means president. Now I don't know much about school, I know all of you want your kids to grow up decent kids with an education so they can live better lives than working from sun up to long after sun down seven days a week . . . And when you educate your children FORGET about taxes—hire the BEST teachers and get the BEST school supplies, the BEST books." And Joe was elected to the school board repeatedly. And Joe's reputation literally blossomed anew from the day he hired out for $15 a month, which was later raised to $30 a month. Eventually Susie's parents died and Susie inherited the farm. Joe and Susie had no children but Joe had no trouble getting hired men. He went to the state reformatory for young men and asked for any young, promising ex-convict from the reformatory. The reformatory was for first time offenders.

Some of those men lasted a day, a week, a month, and some for months. As long as they worked Joe kept them around and treated them well. And he served to rehabilitate quite a number of ex-convicts. When I got my job as state psychologist for Wisconsin to examine all inmates in penal and correctional institutions, Joe was very happy for me, and Joe told me, "There's an old record at the Industrial School that you ought to read, an old record at the reformatory that you ought to read, there's an old record at the state prison that you ought to read." I knew what Joe meant and so I read the Industrial School record. It was very, very violent, Joe had been incorrigible, destructive and brutal in relationship to the other boys there and he had been kept in solitary confinement most of the time from the age of twelve to twenty-one. And his record at Green Bay reformatory was equally black. Joe had been very combative, aggressive. He was kept in solitary, took his meals in solitary. The guards were afraid of him. And when Joe was allowed out of his cell to exercise, two husky guards his size or larger walked through the exercise yard with him . . . one guard ten feet to the right, the other guard ten feet to the left. If Joe were to jump on one of them the second guard would have the chance to jump to the rescue of his fellow guard. The record at the State prison was very, very black. Joe displayed his combativeness, his aggressiveness, his capacity to beat up fellow convicts and he served most of the time in the dungeon. The dungeon was eight feet by eight feet by eight feet, the floor sloped toward the door. It was a very thick, heavy wooden door with a small slot in the door at the base of the door and once a day, usually at one or two A.M. a tray of food would slip quietly through that slot. And once a week the cell was hosed out for sanitation purposes. Now I've been in that dungeon . . . it IS sound proof and light proof. And living in that darkness and silence practically all of his two terms in state prison is pretty severe punishment. And Joe never got a day off. When they did take him out of the dungeon they locked him in a solitary cell. He was exercised by two guards accompanying him, all alone in the exercise yard. Now after the first sentence had been served at the prison, he went to the village and committed robberies and was sent back to the prison and they were all afraid of Joe. And the fellow convicts who I interviewed who knew Joe told me very earnestly, "That Joe is a bad one!" And they were all afraid of him. And all the psychotherapy Joe received was; 'You can if you're a gentleman'. He didn't need psychoanalysis for several years. He didn't need Carl Rogers indirect psychotherapy, he didn't need five years of Gestalt therapy, all he needed was a simple statement . . . 'You can if you're a gentleman'. Psychotherapy has to occur within the patient, everything has to be done by the patient, and the patient has to have a motivation. And so when I became interested in psychiatry Joe's history had a very strong influence on me. You really have to leave the problem of psychotherapy to the patient. You try to understand what your patient is telling you. Your patient has an experiential language all his own and it is different from yours.

And in learning hypnosis myself, I would imagine somebody I knew well and I would suggest hypnosis to that imaginary person and match my words I was using to induce hypnosis against what I knew about them as persons. I am thinking about one subject . . . we worked together with a third person in a peach canning factory. We worked in the warehouse together. I worked there with the other man, first Scotty, then Hal joined us. Now Scotty said "Good morning" when I arrived and "Good night" at the end of the day, so I knew he was a very silent man. So I said only "Good morning, good night" or "there's one more load of cases" or "you better start a new roll" . . . just the ordinary things work required but nothing more. And peach canning became faster, more production, Harold joined us. He started. He said, "Good morning" . . . very silent except for whatever had to be said, but at noon he said, "See you after lunch." After lunch he said, "time to go to work" and "Good evening". Now one day Scotty said to me, "God damn chatter box. I can't stand that fellow Harold jabbering, jabbering, jabbering all day long!" Old Harold just said "See you after lunch—time to go to work."

Which reminds me of a Bret Harte story. Two old prospectors had been prospecting together year after year. And one day one drew his six shooter and shot the other. The authorities asked him why, he said "I'm really a peaceful man. I don't mind him saying Merry Christmas but that chattering of him saying Happy New Year too!! I just couldn't stand it." There is a Bret Harte poem that should be kept in mind by psychotherapists. I can't quote it exactly. "Bean pods rattle best when dry, we always wink with our weakest eye." And an MD I knew took his residency in ophthalmology. He ran across that poem while looking for a subject for his dissertation, "We always wink with our weakest eye." He made a very extensive study with hundreds of people and learned by examination and taking their history that they always learned to wink first with their weakest eye. Bret Harte, a good poet, a good story writer, and a very keen observer of human behavior. Jack Danielson proved it. And there is a lot of things that we do. People with a rural background have no difficulty unlocking my back gate. City dwellers mess it up horribly. It's so simple!!

My first year in college the doctor in charge of student health called me into his office and said, Erickson, you only recently recovered from polio. You've been active as a student and you're doing yourself a lot of damage, and I recommend that you be out in the open getting plenty of exercise and fresh air, eating well and not using your legs at all." I decided that that sounded like a canoe to me. So I purchased a canoe and made a 1200 mile trip down to Lake Madison and the Ohio River and Rock River, the Mississippi just about to St. Louis, and up the Illinois River, headed to the canal, back to Rock River, and back to Madison. I lived on turtle eggs, fish and wild plants and the garbage thrown from the stern wheelers. Whenever they peel a bushel of potatoes they cover up some potatoes and when they dump the potato peelings in the river there would be a potato or two floating on the surface . . . I'd harvest those—same with tomatoes, same with apples. And there are a lot of wild plants that are edible. At first I didn't have anything but a blanket and while I was camping in a pasture alongside the river with my blanket over me it started raining furiously. And that blanket became very heavy. I was wearing a swimming suit, it became very heavy and uncomfortable. I put my head under a fallen log, lay there in the nude, slept peacefully all night. I didn't mind that warm rain. And there were a lot of things that happened on a canoe trip like that. On the Ohio River the water was very clear . . . a school of perch were swimming along under my canoe. I carefully lowered a fish hook on a line. Underneath the fish picked it up until I had a good supply of fish for evening meal and breakfast. Do you know how to cook fish? Well you eviscerate them, wash them, wrap them in plantain leaves (they're wide), and you enclose them in a ball of mud with each end of the ball made thin so steam can burst forth, throw them on top of the camp fire . . . the mud dries out, hardens, the whole thing gets hot, the ends blow out, crack it open, the scales come off with the plantain leaf, and you've got a nice fish freshly

cooked in its own juices . . . add a little salt and eat. Oh
yes, I used my legs a little. I had to get ashore to pick up
wild plants. You have to go out to the sandy island to find
turtle trails to locate a nest full of turtle eggs. A fresh trail
means fresh turtle eggs. And they are very nutritious. I
boiled them in water . . . they are delicious and nutritious.
Of course on the Mississippi I wore my handkerchief
knotted on four corners on my head and just my bathing
suit. I paddled within hailing distance of a fishing boat and
the fishermen would yell, "Hey kid, come over here!"
They were curious about that kid in the canoe. They'd ask
and I said, "I'm a pre-med student at the University of
Wisconsin living in a canoe for the summer getting my
health back." And they always said, "Well what do you
eat??" I'd say, "Fish if I'm lucky, wild plants, potatoes,
tomatoes, and apples the stern wheelers throw out with
the peelings by mistake, turtle eggs." They said, "Well
how about having a fish?" and toss me a nice catfish,
which I promptly returned and said, "Catfish are expen-
sive. That's how you make your living. If you want to give
me a fish, give me a Mississippi perch. It's equally good
eating while a very cheap fish." So they'd toss me a nice
big perch. Also, to set up camp overnight I finally
managed to earn enough money by chopping the mortar
off old bricks for a farmer who lived near the Rock River.
He wanted to build a sugar mill and so he offered me
room and board and so much for a day chopping old
mortar off these second hand bricks. It was easy money.
So I ate well, slept well, and earned money so I was able
to buy a pup tent. And of course I went along the Rock
River, the Mississippi and the Illinois River . . . I always
looked for picnic grounds on the river side to set up camp
within hailing distance of these picnic grounds. All the
kids in the picnic grounds are going to come over to see
what kind of a critter you are. And they'd come over, find

me reading a German book and German was not known in those areas. I'd read it to them, I'd translate for them, they'd rush back and tell their parents all about me—a college student who can read German. The parents would come over, question me. Of course, I inherited all the picnic food they could not eat! It worked out very well. It is amazing the things that happen. One night on the Illinois River I was looking for a place to set up camp, saw a man in a rowboat who was shooting water moccasins. He said, "Are you going to camp anywhere around here?" I said, "Yes, up on the shore." He said, "The water moccasin is a very poisonous snake and they crawl at night. If you're camping on the ground, you'll get bitten." I said, "Thanks" and I watched him kill twenty-two water moccasins and then I picked out my evening's spot —in a nice tree with a nice branch with the right kind of crotch, I put my belt around my waist and the branch, went to sleep lying on the branch of the tree. If I fell off the branch the belt would hold me and I could scramble back. It was a lot of fun traveling like that.

And while I'm telling you each of you are going to relate it so some picnic experience of your own, your childhood, your past, or some particular trip or to some unusual dinner you had. You really don't know how you're going to remember, what I've told you about my canoe trip. Yet you'll remember your own associations. It really doesn't make much difference what you say to a patient. These are conceptions he places upon what you say and that's where the therapy lies.

Now it came time to enter medical school . . . I was without funds and I wondered where I'd find the money. I knew I'd have to work my way. I had my room already paid for a brief period of time and Dr. Clark Hull called me up and said, "The State Board of Control wants to hire a psychologist to do a psychological examination on the inmates of the Correctional and Penal Institute of Wisconsin. It's a good job. It is only a part time job, and I can't find a psychologist who wants it. I know you want to go to medical school and that you have no funds, so you might look into the job." I took the job . . . and earned my way through medical school . . . I have my own ways of doing things. To get a master's degree I knew I'd have enough hours by the time I got my MD to qualify for a master's degree . . . and to get a master's degree you had to write a dissertation. Now, while working in a prison population I learned a lot of things about criminals and crime. And I wrote up some of those findings in a paper which I published, and the medical school approved it as a dissertation for a master's degree. And one other experience—a learning experience—the State Board of Control ordered me a highly technical, statistical job one summer. The pay was excellent. I never had a course in statistics and I had to do correlation coefficients and make a statistical study of crime and criminals. So I asked Dr. Hull for the best book on statistics and he said, "Ewell is the best book but you won't even be able to read it much less understand it." I said, "That'll be my problem." I bought the book. I read it through very carefully . . . word by word. It was the darnedest mishmash I ever read. So I read it through a second time . . . and I'll be darned, somehow it made sense to me. And in all I read that book through seven times, and by the time I read it through seven times I knew all about statistics. I could take on that job—a whole summer's employment. Once the Board of Control wanted some correlation figures in relationship to criminals. They had four-digit numbers that needed correlating. I was informed about that possibility Saturday noon. I was told the order had to be on the Board of Control president's desk Monday morning and you can imagine doing one thousand correlation coefficients. Well I've always believed in looking ahead, so I volunteered in taking the assignment. I knew I couldn't do all that scoring, dividing, multiplying, addition and so on. I knew there was an adding machine in the psychology department. I carefully went up, went through that window carefully left unlocked, borrowed the adding machine, took it to my room. And I knew that the square root of 169 is 13, but how do you get the square root on an adding machine? All mathematics is addition or subtraction, so is extracting the square root a matter of addition or subtraction. So I played around with the keys until I could get the square root of 169. I already knew the answer but what keys do you press in order to get the answer 13? So I took a four digit number which I knew the square root and worked out how to do that. I spent all Saturday afternoon working out the use of the adding machine, extracting the square root and so on. Monday morning one thousand correlation coefficients were on the Board of Controller's desk. Why should I say I couldn't do it? All mathmetics is plus or add, plus or subtract. And an adding machine can do it much more rapidly than a pen or pencil and much more accurately. Now people should not assume they can't do things until they look at the thing in a simplified way and decide what they can really do, because they can usually do a lot more than they think they can do.

Now it brings me to mind in medical school in the physiology laboratory . . . the students were divided up into groups of four. Each group was given a rabbit. We were requested to do various things, including an intravenous injection, and Dr. Meakson said, "Anybody that has a rabbit die gets a zero" . . . Our rabbit died. Dr. Meakson looked at it and said, "Sorry boys, you get a zero." I said, "Sorry Dr. Meakson, the autopsy had not yet been done." So we did an autopsy, asked him to examine it, and he said, "With all that sarcosis that rabbit didn't have a right to be alive. You boys get an A!"

When I first went to Massachusetts in the 1930's there was the most traditional place in the world, everything followed tradition very rigidly. I joined the hospital staff. I was introduced the first morning—one doctor was absent. I rode up and down the elevator with him for three months. I always said "Good morning" "Good afternoon" or "Good evening," but he hadn't been properly introduced to me so he couldn't reply. And in the first meeting of the New England Society a psychiatrist and I attended. I was astonished at what I saw!! There were men dressed in tuxedos. I asked why. The psychiatrist explained either they were giving a paper or they were going to discuss a paper. According to my foreign ways of thinking you didn't have to have a tuxedo. So Pete Campbell, the dean of psychiatry in New England at that time, a very wonderful man, presented a paper on hypnosis. And he finished. I got up and asked for permission to discuss the paper. The Society went into the state of shock. They had to recess. And then they resumed the meeting and explained that since I was foreign to the ways of the East it would be all right for me to discuss Dr. Campbell's paper. So I spoke more freely . . . my opening statement was something to the effect, "I thought Dr. Campbell owed an apology to the Society to the people in attendance for the sophomoric paper on hypnosis. It was carelessly prepared, superficial, poorly organized." A state of shock for everyone. Pete Campbell got up and said, "I agree with Dr. Erickson. I was very careless and I knew Dr. Erickson's writings. I know of him and I want to apologize to him and all of you. The next time that I present a paper I will present a well done paper." Pete Campbell and I became very close friends.

I'll give you a personal example of improving memory
. . . in Michigan I was a professor of psychiatry and
director of the psychiatric research and training at Wayne
County Hospital. A lawyer's son in Chicago, who had a
PhD and an MD degree, was a psychiatrist. And he had
had experience in criminal psychiatry and his PhD was
in psychology. He also had two master degrees and two
bachelor degrees—all totaled, six earned University degree. And he applied for a job as a psychiatric consultant
for the criminal court in Detroit, dealing with criminals,
traffic problems and so on. And the lawyer's son was
hired on the strength of his experiences. He wasn't interviewed. The criminal court decided a man with all those
degrees, training in criminal psychiatry and general psychiatry was the right man. And Lyle arrived. And Lyle
took over his office. And his office was in the state of
severe shock because Lyle knew everything about everything and all of the people were inferior, very inferior!!
After he got his office in order, he went to Wayne State
University, explained to the Psychology Department that
Dr. Skaggs, head of the department, was getting old, he
might as well retire and HE, Lyle, would take Dr. Skaggs
place also . . . as an incidental position. He went to the
medical school, explained to the Dean he had a lot more
degrees than I had, why not drop me from the faculty,
and he'd take up my duties. Now that's bad enough. He
visited the office of every private psychiatrist in Detroit
and told patients in the waiting room 'you really ought to
see a good psychiatrist' and named him. And he also
went to the Detroit Free Press and explained to them how
often he wanted a feature story on him. He was a very
obese man. He rapidly got the name 'little Lyle'. And at
the end of a week, he looked at his secretary that he had
inherited—a Civil Service employee—and said, "Miss X,
you rather have a dumpy figure, you're prematurely gray,

you're very plain featured, you're cross-eyed . . . I wouldn't mind having you for a mistress for a month or so." She was so infuriated she quit! I was looking for a secretary at the time and since my secretary was on the Civil Service, she was transfered to me. That was in early spring of '42. And in August of '42 the city of Detroit became electrified. Lyle had written a seventeen page, single line, typewritten letter to the Army explaining why they should commission him as General to look after the mental health of the other Generals. And the Army's reply was, "Dear Sir, At this time we have no use of a man with your talents." His psychological assistant was in the office. Little Lyle didn't have the sense NOT to show what poor judgment the Army had and he read the seventeen page letter to his staff, showed them the Army's reply, and spoke disparagingly about the intelligence of the Army. The psychologist quietly abstracted the carbon copy of the letter and the Army's reply and took it to the newspaper. And it came out with the headline: "Army Says It Has No Use for Lyle". And that was in August. And my secretary coming back from lunch saw the noon day edition with that headline, she promptly bought it and told me about it, about the incident . . . she brought it up and showed me the headline and said, "Let's call up 'little Lyle' and weep crocodile tears." I said, "Go ahead if you want to call him up and weep crocodile tears. It is perfectly all right, he deserves them . . . but when *I* SHAFT 'little Lyle', it will be a shafting that he'll never forget!!!" I had no plans—August passed, September passed, October passed. The later part of November there was a meeting at the Wayne County Medical Society Building in Detroit and I attended. And the early arrivals, including me, were inside drinking punch. In walked "little Lyle". The first person he saw when he opened the door was me, he said, "Hi Milt, what do you know?'' And I said, "All I know is what I read in newspapers" (Will Rogers' famous line). I knew my unconscious mind was intelligent and I could rely upon it to say the right thing, do the right thing at the right moment and Lyle furnished the right stimulus, and the vast accumulation of knowledge I had in my unconscious immediately selected the right one. Soon as the other doctors heard that reply they dropped their glasses on the table and rushed to the telephone . . . of course the newspaper came out with another headline: "ERICKSON TELLS LYLE IS ALL HE KNOWS IS WHAT HE READS IN THE NEWSPAPER." And 'little Lyle' moved to Florida. I shafted him, but very sweetly, just by using an item of common information. I always trust my unconscious. Now too many psychotherapists try to plan what thinking they will do instead of waiting to see what the stimulus they receive is and then letting their unconscious mind respond to that stimulus.

I took my degree in Wisconsin and interned in Colorado because I knew that medicine was viewed differently in different parts of the country. I learned that arthritis in Colorado was very, very different than it was in Wisconsin. I also learned that when you used ether in Colorado you poured it on instead of dropping it on. I next went to Rhode Island, I found out that you are very careful and very slow in dropping ether on the cone. Colorado is way above sea level, and in the East medicine was practiced differently for different diseases than in Wisconsin or Colorado. I expect there is much less difference in the States now. I think each patient you see should be a challenge where you recognize the individuality of the patient. And I think you ought to spend your free time going swimming, or fishing, or dancing, and watching other people . . . find out how much information your eyes can give you about that person, so long as

that person is a stranger to you. Now we grow up with
seeing and hearing and we regard that as all we have to
do. Yet when you get acquainted with a blind person he
HEARS.

In teaching medical students I give long lectures to the
effect they do some outside reading. And I point to a
certain book case and I would tell them there is a book
on Human Laterality and I would ask one of the students
to go and find that book in that case and I'd explain "It
has the title *Human Laterality* printed on it very plainly
and there is no mistaking the book. It is a hard cover and
brilliant red in color." And then I let him go to the book
case to let him find the book while the class is watching.
And some of the students with vision good enough could
locate that title and would be surprised when their class-
mates went right past that book. After he had searched
the book case repeatedly not being able to find that bright
red hard-cover book entitled *Human Laterality,* I would
tell them to "look in the upper left hand corner of the top
shelf and read the titles, one by one, until he found the
book, that bright red book, entitled *Human Laterality.*"
And he would read each title, including *Human Laterality,* and go on to the next book, because when he read
Human Laterality without attaching any meaning to it.
And then when he read perhaps the titles twice and
declared, emphatically, that book was not there, then I
would tell another student, "Go and pick out in the bookcase the book called *Human Laterality* it's blue," and
he'd find the book easily because it WAS a hard covered
blue colored book. Now that classmate had searched for
that book with a certain frame of reference and that frame
of reference included a hard cover, a bright red color and
the two words *Human Laterality.* Those are distinctive
words, they were only a mere *part* of the frame of reference in which he was searching and hence they were

separate and did not form a part of a red colored, hard covered book frame of reference. Just reading the two words was not sufficient, and we do that all the time in our life experiences. We are blind to things, we fail to hear things, we fail to feel things, we fail to smell things, we fail to taste things. We fail to recognize kinesthetic sensations, proprioceptive sensations, and that's *part* of living. As for your conscious living you tend to select certain parts and remain unaware of other things. And in hypnotic trance you can in an intentional way, without knowing it, so direct your attention that you can see people with your eyes closed, you can hear people talking in the room that is entirely silent, you can transport yourself in thought from California, to Maine, and listen to the sound of the ocean waves on the coast even if you've never heard ocean waves . . .

Now one year at medical school at the beginning of the year the dean called me into the office and said, "I'm new here." He came from Minnesota. "I brought with me a protege student. He is a genius in pathology. He is unusually talented and dedicated to the science of pathology. And he hates psychiatrists with a passion. And he will go out of his way to aggravate you, insult you, antagonize you in every possible way." I said, "All right, I'll take care of the boy." So the first lecture I made my usual introduction to the class: "I'm not the ordinary medical school professor who thinks his course is the only important course. I'm not that kind of professor, I just KNOW the course I'm teaching is the most important." The first time I pulled that on them the entire class signed a petition to have me dropped from the faculty. The dean showed me the petition. I said give it to me and three weeks later I posted it on the blackboard and never made reference to it, delivered my lecture. So usually in the first lecture period I explain, of course, what psychiatry was and I thought they all ought to do some outside reading. I named a half dozen books that those who were really interested in psychiatry would find interesting and that really the whole class ought to read outside, and I listed about thirty more books, and some of them might also be interesting reading. And then I gave them an assignment. "the next Monday morning at eight o'clock you all hand in a review of certain book of psychiatry." And that protege of the dean gave me a hard look. The next morning they lined up passing in their reviews and he was grinning from ear to ear, handed me a blank sheet of paper. I said, "Without reading it I've noticed you've made two mistakes. You've failed to date it and you haven't signed it. So next Monday when you hand it in bear in mind that a book review is like a report on a pathological slide." The next week he handed in one of the best book reviews I've ever read. And a couple of weeks later the dean said, "How in the world did you ever make a Christian out of that heathen?" He was all set to antagonize me thoroughly. I went right along with it and pointed out his two mistakes. And he had to admit them.

Now an instance of using your own unconscious mind —I was writing a paper, a publication and I thought I had it finished. This was in November. And one day I decided to send it to the publishers but I couldn't find that paper. I knew I kept my manuscript in one of four different places. I looked at all four places . . . the manuscript wasn't there, so I said, "My unconscious mind is trying to tell me something, I wonder what?" November passed, December, January. A new group of medical students arrived for second semester and so I assigned them to the books they ought to read, showed them the bookcase in my office, and picked up some books casually and said, "Here is a book you really ought to read."

I opened it at random and THERE WAS A REFERENCE that belonged in my manuscript!! After the medical students left I unlocked the bottom drawer of my desk, pulled out my lost manuscript, added that reference. Now my unconscious knew that I would have a new group of medical students, my unconscious knew how I always began each semester, and my unconscious knew that there was no hurry about getting that paper published and it would be more complete.

I had a similar experience in Arizona. I had completed a paper and I thought it was a very excellent paper and I decided to mail it. So I looked for it and I couldn't find it in any of the four places I kept my manuscripts. So I said, "I wonder what I omitted from that paper?" About a month later a patient came in for her monthly check-up. She entered the room, I pulled out the file, took out her case record—there was my manuscript. So I asked that patient some questions I had overlooked asking her—a lot of new information that I added to that paper. You rely on your unconscious mind.

Years ago I tried to write a paragraph of explanation . . . I have forgotten what it concerned. Some time after I wrote that paragraph I found it unsatisfactory because it didn't express the meaning I wanted to express. So one day I have two hours free, I said, 'I think I'll just lean back and go into a trance.' About an hour and forty-five minutes later, here in my lap, was a box of comic books and on my desk were two piles of comic books. And a patient due very soon. I wondered why I had gone into a trance and looked through a box of comic books and why I'd leave two different piles of comic books on my desk. In anticipation of the patient, I put all the comic books back in the box, took them out into the other room. Came back and my patient arrived and I proceeded to interview the patient. And I forgot about that evidence of self-hypnosis and the discovery of a box of comic books in my lap. And one day I had some free time and I thought about writing that explanation and it was a little bit difficult for me. I picked up a pencil and it came into my mind 'And Huey duck said to Louie duck . . .' Then I realized—comic books appeal to all levels of intelligence and they do convey a lot of meaning. And comic books have to be precise and very clear and I wrote that explanation that I wanted to write with the greatest of ease. My unconscious had me examine comic books to get an awareness of conciseness and simplicity.

And one thing that all children teach you is that there are different ways of looking at things. My daughter, Betty Alice, as a toddler was on the hospital grounds at Wayne County Hospital, Michigan. And wandered around looking this way that way, here and there, and she'd double up and look at the scenery from between her legs looking here there and everywhere. And she surveyed the entire hospital grounds that way standing upright and then bent double. I didn't know what it meant then. And when she was a little over five years old I brought Gregory Bateson home from Evanston where we had been at a Psychological meeting. Bateson is six feet four or six feet six tall. Betty Alice's full growth is five feet two. And that little girl walked around and around him, looked up at that man with the head in the sky. And she managed to see that he pay attention to her, she told him how many miles it was to the moon, how many miles it was to Mars, Venus, Pluto and too gave him all the distances. I didn't know where she picked them up be she had them. And I didn't recognize the significance THEN. Then she demanded to know where Gregory came from. He said Australia. She took ahold of the globe, asked him to locate Australia. He located Australia and showed her where Michigan was. And she announced very solemnly, "When I grow up I am going to go to Australia." After her schooling in Michigan, took a job teaching and the next summer went traveling over Europe. Came back taught in Michigan and toured the United States the following summer. Dropped by here and said, "I thought I'd tell you folks, drop in to see you folks before I left for Australia. I'm teaching school there." Now she's taught school in Michigan, Arizona, Australia, Ethiopia and now teaching school in Okinawa and looking forward to her husband's new assignment somewhere else in the world. Her interest in seeing things from every possible point of view, her interest in distances signified in advance that she would be a traveler and see things. She's traveled over Ethiopia in a balloon, down in rafts in the river with hippopotami and crocodiles. And she's been to Korea, Hong Kong, planning a trip to China, she's been to Singapore, of course Hawaii, I don't know what many places. And her family, her two sons and daughter, they always take their roots with them. And wherever they hang their hat—they put down their roots. And they're as secure as they can be.

Children have short memories and I'll tell you how to teach children to have good memories. My son Robert one evening announced that he was big enough, old enough, strong enough to take out the garbage. I expressed my doubts, he assured me he WAS big enough, strong enough. I said he might forget, he assured me he wouldn't. I said, "All right beginning Monday you can do it." So Monday night he took it out, Tuesday night he took it out and Wednesday night he forgot. So I reminded him on Thursday he apologized for forgetting on Wednesday —took it out Thursday night but forgot it Friday and Saturday. It just happened that early on Sunday morning at 3 A.M. I awakened. I had been very good to Robert—I had let him stay up till past one o'clock. I had awakened at three o'clock. I had wakened Robert apologized very profusely for not having reminded him for taking out the garbage—would he please dress, take out the garbage. So Robert with many unknown thoughts sighed deeply—dressed—took out the garbage. Came back in got out of his clothes into his pajamas into bed. I waited till he was very sound asleep—I awakened him—apologized very sincerely, very profusely, explaining I didn't know how that one piece of garbage got overlooked. Robert made a more extensive minute search of the kitchen took that piece of garbage out to the garbage pail walked back to the house slowly. I was watching through the curtained window. He reached the back porch turned and ran out the alley and kicked off the cover off the garbage can. He came in and thoughtfully undressed into his pajamas. I never again had to remind him. I've pulled that trick on all my kids, eight kids got similar memory lessons. That's a nice way to improve your memory.

I entered a hotel in Miami, Florida in the dining room and a waiter handed me a menu in French. I explained that I didn't read French and with a horribly thick French accent he offered to translate it. So I enjoyed having him read each item but I couldn't even understand 't'aire'. When he finished I said, "Would you please bring me a glass of cracked ice." He looked puzzled but he brought a glass of cracked ice. I said, "Now bring me a bottle of french dressing." He looked even more puzzled. I took the bottle, poured the dressing over the cracked ice and said, "Now put this in the garbage pail." He said, "Yes sir" and I exited through the door. Two years later I was in a dining room in a hotel in Portland, Oregon. The waiter said, "Good evening, Dr. Erickson." I said, "Obviously you know me. I have a very poor memory for faces." He said, "Yes we've met before and before the evening is over you'll remember." I said "That's fine." I got the most remarkably competent service. He brought the check. I put the bills on it. He brought the change. I left a tip and thanked him for the good service. And he bade me good night in the thickest French accent.

Now, a child who's never been in a swimming pool . . . You know, it's a very questionable thing to step into a swimming pool . . . all the way down those steps at the shallow end. Your body FEELS so different. First TIME you go into the water, the water reaches your chest level, you come to discover it's difficult to breathe. You haven't got the ordinary body pressures. Got a new set of pressures. And, ducking UNDER the water . . . oh that's terrifying. Yet you can get kids to bob for apples in the bathtub. And pretty soon the kids will be so desperate they'll grab a hold of an apple and force it down to the bottom of the tub and get a good grip on it. And get over their fear of having their head under water. They assume they were only playing a game . . . they were learning.

AFTERWARDS

N ow, therapy should not be a massive job. Your clients know what
they need . . . but they don't always KNOW that they know.
You provide them with a situation in which they can discover it, you
keep their attention on the road. I'll give you an example of that. I
had been conducting one of my teaching seminars here in Phoenix.
It was the end of the last day for that particular group and I was tired
. . . I had given them what they'd come for and more. So, I called Betty
on the intercom to come get me. While we waited, the group became
more and more restless . . . No child likes to come in from play. Finally,
David and Maribeth asked to take some photographs. They said they
wanted to show their children, their grandchildren. I smiled and
nodded in agreement. David took the helm and wheeled me out under
the Palo Verde tree. They stood behind my wheelchair, trying to act
nonchalant, while the photographer focused and recorded their dis-
tress. Then it was time for them to take their departure, but they
hesitated, looking this way and that . . . they thought that it was to
be a FINAL farewell. But the seeds that I had planted would grow
and keep growing long after they left Phoenix. *I* knew that, but at the
time they didn't. I released the brake on my chair. Maribeth fluttered
and said, "Dr. Erickson", leaned her head forward, then reached for

my hand. She started to say, "I want to thank you . . .", but I said, "You're a coward!! And I have proof!" Oh, she was aghast—speechless! I *knew* she knew, but SHE didn't know she knew. And I said, "You're unconscious knows and so do *you,*" and I turned to glare at David . . . he looked shell-shocked. Then they both said good-bye, hesitated, then leaned forward, and kissed me on the cheek.

BIBLIOGRAPHY

Bandler, R. and Grinder, J. *Patterns of the Hypnotic Techniques of Milton H. Erickson, M.D., Vol. I,* Meta Publications, Cupertino, Ca 1975.

Bandler, R. and Grinder, J. *The Structure of Magic, Vol. I.* Science and Behavior Books, Palo Alto, Ca 1975.

Bandler, R. and Grinder, J. *Frogs Into Princes,* Real People Press, Moab, Utah 1979.

Cameron-Bandler, L. *They Lived Happily Ever After,* Meta Publications, Cupertino, Ca 1978.

Dilts, R., J. Grinder, L. Cameron-Bandler, R. Bandler, and J. Delozier *Neuro-Linguistic Programming, Vol. I,* Meta Publications, Cupertino, Ca 1980.

Gordon, D. *Therapeutic Metaphors,* Meta Publications, Cupertino, Ca 1978.

Grinder, J. and Bandler, R. *The Structure of Magic II,* Science and Behavior Books, Palo Alto, Ca 1976.

Grinder, J., Delozier, J. and Bandler, R. *Patterns of the Hypnotic Techniques of Milton H. Erickson, M.D. Vol. II,* Meta Publications, Cupertino, Ca 1977.

Haley, J. (ed.) *Advanced Techniques of Hypnosis and Therapy,* Grune and Stratton, New York 1967.

Haley, J. *Uncommon Therapy,* Grune and Stratton, New York 1973.

Zeig, J. (ed.) *A Teaching Seminar with Milton H. Erickson,* Brunner/Mazel, New York 1980.